U.S. DEMOCRACY SEVERELY IN DANGER!

YOU BE THE JUDGE

by Robert Lee Davis

DORRANCE
PUBLISHING CO
EST. 1920
PITTSBURGH, PENNSYLVANIA 15238

Dorrance Publishing Co
585 Alpha Drive
Suite 103
Pittsburgh, PA 15238
Visit our website at *www.dorrancebookstore.com*

ISBN: 979-8-8852-7141-7
eISBN: 979-8-8852-7868-3

CONTENTS

INTRODUCTION

The Purpose of this book is written based on two major grounds: First Ground is to Discuss Criminal Actions against our Nation's Democratic Principles, which is required by federal law Pursuant to Title 18 U.S.C. Section 2382, and Second is to give a bird's eye view of the dangerous treasonous acts committed by a federal District Court judge, in the person of Judge Terrance W. Boyle, who sets on the bench for the Eastern District of North Carolina, Southern Division, as demonstrated in the Following pages of this Book, which provides a descriptive and analytical thirty-year history of insurrection against the United States Articles and Constitution committed by the above named federal judge and who appears to be the spokesman on behalf of several federal judges based on the fact that Boyles's dangerous and treasonous assault upon the Constitution of the United States, which are clearly identified within the pages of this book and included with conspiracy with two North Carolina Court Judges, whose names are Russell G. Walker and G. Bryan Collins Jr. Furthermore, the most important Purpose of this book is to provide the readers with the fact that the same insurrection remains in action during the development of this book, even though those actions of insurrection have been reported to the United States Attorney General, Merrick Garland, on or about March 30, 2021, with authentic documented evidence. The Attorney General in turn has passed those descriptive criminal actions over with the Federal Bureau of Investigation (FBI), which appears to support the Attorney General's statement made during his Senate Confirmation Hearing for the Office of which he now occupies: "NO ONE IS ABOVE THE LAW." Therefore, much of the information cited in this book is basically the same provided to the United States Department of Justice and Supported by Statement Under Penalty of Contempt Pursuant to United States Title 18 U.S.C. Section 1746. A copy of that above said Criminal Report is included in this book with appropriate attachments as evidence for viewing of the reader listed as attachment "A." No Crime should be engaged against our government in absence of a report to the proper source and made to the American People. Therefore, the Reader can see the listed crimes which places Judge Terrance W. Boyle well under the United States Statute Pursuant to 18 U.S.C. Sec. 2382, and under such circumstance, clear grounds are established for impeachment as has been the case in past years with fifteen judges of whom eight of those judges were proven to be guilty, and removed from office; four were found not guilty; and three of those judges resigned before an outcome at trial. More details of those Fifteen Judges are discussed in pages listed below; therefore, it would be interesting should the reader compare the criminal Conduct of Judge Terrance W. Boyle in comparison with some or all of those Fifteen Judges as to the Criminal treasonous acts engaged by Judge Terrance W. Boyle and along with those state judges whom Judge Boyle conspired with as a sitting judge while hardworking citizens are paying his high salary and his appointment is unlimited as a sitting judge on the federal bench. Rather than upholding the integrity of our Nation's Constitutional Judicial System, the named federal judge wages acts of Treasons against our Democratic Institutions.

Davis, the Author of this Book, entitled *US DEMOCRACY SEVERELY IN DANGER: YOU BE THE JUDGE*, has provided enough information regarding those fifteen impeached federal judges under which the reader may reach the level of belief that Judge Terrance W. Boyle should be impeached and removed from office, and if that be the case, the reader may want to call his or her Congressional Representative for purpose of protecting the Democratic institutions of the United States. One of the most important questions that may be raised to one's Congressional Representative, "If Judge Terrance W. Boyle is not placed before the United States House of Representatives for an impeachment hearing and possible go there from to the United States Senate for trial, should this process go without activation?" The question to be raised, "Why not, since it is made known to the Fact that Judge Terrance W. Boyle is Not Above the Law?" And the factors that add to Judge Terrance W. Boyle's treasonous acts upon our nation's Constitution is to the fact that several appellate federal judges support Judge Boyle's criminal action, which is without a doubt proven to the reader of this book. Therefore, "YOU BE THE JUDGE."

CHARGE OF TREASON AND MISPRISION OF TREASON INCLUDED WITH SEVERAL INCIDENTS OF PERJURY AMONG OTHER CRIMINAL ACTS BY JUDGE TERRANCE W. BOYLE ENGAGED WHILE ABSENCE OF ALL JURISDICTION

First, the Author will set forth the direct words expressed by the United States Supreme Court regarding a judge exercising his actions without jurisdiction. "We (Judges) have no more right to decline the exercise of jurisdiction which is given than to usurp that which is not given. The one or the other would be treason to the Constitution." Cited in cases *US v. Will*, 449 U.S. 200, 216, 101 S.Ct. 471, 66 L.Ed.2d 1392, 406 (1980); *Cohens v. Virginia*, 19 U.S. (6 Wheat) 264, 404, 5 L. Ed 257 (1821).

On or about April 23, 2001, a panel of judges of the Seventh Circuit Court of Appeals said, "Napoleon at his coronation took the imperial crown out of the hands of the Pope and crowned himself. Federal judges do not have a similar prerogative. A court that does not have jurisdiction cannot assume it, however worthy the cause." Case No. 00-4267, In Brand Name Prescription Drugs Antitrust Litigation, Appeal of: William Mack Price, et. al.

In addition, Judge Terrance W. Boyle acted on two different occasions in absent of Jurisdiction: 1. His power to protect North Carolina Superior Court Judge Russell G. Walker, who was a sitting judge on North Carolina State Judicial District 19 and, without having been given an assignment as required by law, took it upon himself and came into North Carolina State Judicial District 16 and illegally forced Davis into a Robeson County Superior Court to be tried for a crime of which was never filed against Davis; no warrant was ever served upon Davis, and at that trial, Illegal Judge Russell G. Walker prevented Davis from contacting his lawyer and Judge Walker testified against Davis to the jury with incriminating Statements which amounted to Perjury as to those inflatory statements made to the jury from the lips of Judge Russell G. Walker in absent of all jurisdiction.

Federal District Court Judge Terrance W. Boyle stepped outside of his jurisdiction to protect and did protect two of North Carolina Superior Court Judges whose names are Judge Russell G. Walker and Superior Court Judge G. Bryan Collins Jr., which gave birth to the felonious crimes of Conspiracy, which are discussed in Attachment "A."

As a matter of fact, all documents of evidence are attached to Attachment "A" as Exhibits.

In addition to the subject named judge's insurrection with Perjury, treasonous acts, neglect of his legal and statutory duty, malfeasance, misfeasance, and nonfeasance and Judge Terrance W. Boyle's conspiracy with North Carolina Superior Court Judges Russell G. Walker and G. Bryan Collins.

First, it is essential to demonstrate the unlawful conspiracy of Federal District Court Judge Terrance W. Boyle in an alliance with North Carolina State Superior Court Judge Russell G. Walker's acts of aggression against the Amendments and Constitution of the United States. As Judge Boyle clearly engaged conspiracy in conjunction with North Carolina Superior Court Judge Russell G. Walker, who unlawfully engaged treasonous acts against North Carolina Constitution and the Constitution of the United States in which federal judge Terrance W. Boyle demonstrated in his unlawful conduct in conspiracy to hide, and Schiele, the unlawful conduct of North Carolina Superior Court Judge Russell G. Walker, which is in itself a federal crime based on the United States Supreme Court ruling holding "that a judge does not have jurisdiction to protect and encourage perjury to prevent response to opposing party such as a joint conspiracy to block the orderly function by croupily testifying on behalf of a litigant while at the same time presiding as judge." The name of the case which the Supreme Court issued its Ruling: *Ferri v. Kerman*, 444 U.S. 193 (1979).

As related to Judge Terrance W. Boyle's Lies (Committed Perjury) under his Oath to hide and Schiele State Superior Court Judge Russell G. Walker in Davis's lawsuit *Davis v. Walker*, case file No. 7: 98-CV-116, Judge Boyle's Perjury was put forth in his Order protecting Judge Walker, saying that he entertained the issues in the above-named case. These were the issues that were set forth in the above-named Lawsuit: a) Judge Walker, unlawful, came from his Judicial District 19 and assigned himself to enter Judicial District 16 for purpose to have Davis under his illegal judgeship in a criminal trial. Judge Boyle had full knowledge that no judge anywhere in the United States is allowed to enter a different Judicial District without a Certificate of Assignment, and when a judge comes into a different Judicial District without an assignment, that judge loses his jurisdiction; by the same token, that judge become an ordinary citizen, and the truth of the matter, an ordinary citizen cannot preside over any matter regarding the judicial system within the United States. Therefore, Judge Walker acted as a judge without jurisdiction and, therefrom, engaged in an act of treason: *US vs. Will*, 449 U.S. 200, 216, 101 S. Ct. 471, 66 L.Ed. 2d 392, 406 (1980); *Chens v. Virginia*, 19 U.S. (6 Wheat) 264,404, L.Ed 257 (1821).

Judge Boyle knew, or should have known, of the fact that the United States Supreme Court has issued a ruling which says, "Engaging in an act of treason against the United States Constitution by any citizen of the United States is an act of war against the United States," *Cooper v. Aaron*, 358 U.S. 1, 78 S. Ct 1401 (1958). It is interesting to note that those issues have been put before Judge Terrence W. Boyle by letter from Davis and filed in court documents—See Document A. Therefore, Judge Boyle has not denied a single criminal fact set out against him. However, Judge Boyle lied to protect two of North Carolina superior Court Judges.

To make matters clear regarding the insurrection of Judge Boyle, the following facts must be considered: Ruled under Perjury contempt by saying in an Order that he considered all issues listed in Davis above named Civil Lawsuit; Committed Perjury Number One, Judge Boyle said nothing about Judge Walker's Criminal act of holding a criminal tried without Jurisdiction; Criminal Perjury Number Two, Judge Boyle said nothing of Davis having been forced into a Criminal trial without haven been served with an arrest Warrant and not having been charged of any crime; Perjury Number Three, Judge Boyle said nothing of Davis haven being denied an attorney at the unlawful criminal court trial; Perjury Number Four, Judge Boyle said nothing regarding

Davis was ordered to a criminal trial less than twenty-four hours without prior notice; Perjury Number Five, Judge Boyle said nothing regarding Judge Walker permitting a fifteen-year-old girl, Jamie Michelle Floyd, to lie on the witness stand, claiming that she got so sick regarding the lie about indecent exposure which she claimed to have happened on March 19, 1992, and not given no specific place where the accused indecent exposure supposed to have happen other than just saying it happened in Biggs Park, which is a relative large parking lot, further saying she missed many days out of school, had to go to the hospital, she had to see a doctor and a psychiatrist, of which were authentically proven to be lies of which Davis Conducted his own investigation with volunteer help of others following his illegal Prosecution. Furthermore, Jamie Michell Floyd's 1992–93, School attendance Record is listed in this book and the reader can and will be observe to the fact that Jamie Floyd did not miss a day out of school following the dates of March 17 through the last day of that School Year. Again, Jamie Floyd's school attendance record is provided in this book—See Document "A." Furthermore, there is absolutely no evidence of Jamie Floyd ever having to visit a hospital, never visiting a doctor nor a psychiatrist as the young teenage girl testified under oath as to Davis's illegal court trial.

At this point, Davis will raise several questions which may arrive in the mind of the Reader: One, Why is it that Davis did not get that information before his trial? Answer: Davis was forced into the criminal trial less than twenty-four hours before the criminal trial was held, and within that twenty-four-hour period, Davis filed a handwritten Motion for Discovery in the Clerk's office, and Judge Walker wrote his Order of denial on Davis's Handwritten Motion—See Document "A"; and Two, Were there legitimate Judges in Judicial District 16? Answer: Yes, those Judges would not engage in such criminal action, and as a resort, Judge Russell Walker assigned himself to hold the illegal court trial without Jurisdiction to the satisfaction of Davis's accusers, and by law, Russell Walker was not a judge and served as a judge under false pretense.

Jamie Floyd's Father, Phillip Floyd, also lied under oath on the Witness Stand, who had testified prior to his daughter, Jamie Michell Floyd. The Court transcript is made available of Phillip Floyd's Perjured testimony under oath at trial—See Document "A" Phillip Floyd's Perjured Testimony. Perjury Number Six, Judge Boyle said nothing about Judge Walker denied Davis Discovery for purpose to see what if anything he was charged with, and who would testify against him; Perjury Number Seven, Judge Boyle said nothing about Judge Walker telling the Jury just before the jurors went to the Jury room for deliberation in which Walker told the Jury: "Ladies and gentlemen, the Court has ruled that in the instance of this case, under all the evidence, Mr. Davis voluntarily went with the officers to the police department and, there from, went voluntarily to the magistrate's office to appear before the magistrate; under those circumstances no arrest was made and no arrest warrant was required under the law of the State of North Carolina." See Court Transcript listed in Attachment "A." The said statement made to the Jury was an act of Perjury under Judge Walker's Oath and in absence of Jurisdiction to set on a court bench. A copy of the Court Transcript with Judge Walker's Perjured Statements made to the Jury is available in this book. Judge Russell G. Walker should have been arrested and brought before a just Court. Nevertheless, Judge Walker had a Federal District Court Judge to protect him and did so with the force of Perjury. Judge Boyle's Perjury and Judge Terrance Boyle did not say a word about Davis's issue regarding his illegal imprisonment resulting from that illegal trial; Judge Boyle said nothing regarding Davis's long period of probation and five-hundred-dollar fine imposed upon Davis. See Judge Boyle's action listed concerning the affect regarding Davis's teaching career.

Those acts of Perjury were committed as a resort to the fact that Federal Judge Boyle, under perjury, claimed that he had analyzed all issues regarding the treasonous crimes committed by Judge Russell Walker.

First, as a matter of proof, it is essential to show the coldhearted, calculated crimes committed by North Carolina Superior Court Judge Russell G. Walker in his Treasonous action against the Amendments to the Federal Constitution and doing so knowingly to the fact with complete knowledge of his treasonous action.

Now, it is the time and Purpose to show proof with solid evidence supported by Genuine and Authentic Documents, of which will support the grounds as to the Eight Engagements of PERJURY.

STAGE ONE

BACKGROUND: DATES AND TIME
BASED ON THE FOLLOWING SPECIFIC FACTS BELOW REEMPHASIZED BASED ON THE SERIOUS CRIMES COMMITTED BY JUDGES

The facts are listed in support of the information provided above. In other words, the information provided above standing alone would be without much meaning. Therefore, Davis provides his Background consisting of DATES AND TIME.

Now, here we go: Federal District Judge Terrance W. Boyle engaged a Felonious Conspiracy with North Carolina State Superior Court Judge Russell G Walker.

On April 13, 1993, a North Carolina State Superior Court Judge, Russell G. Walker, Presiding Judge on North Carolina Judicial District Nineteen, unlawfully came to North Carolina Judicial District Sixteen without having been designated by North Carolina Administrative Office of the Courts and forced Davis into a criminal trial for a crime of indecent exposure which Davis did not committee, neither was Davis ever charged in a warrant of such a crime nor any other crime as required by state and federal constitutional law, no criminal action was ever reported to a law enforcement office; Davis was denied discovery, denied an attorney, allowed a police officer named Don Ward, who happened to have been in the Courtroom on the day of the unlawful trial; Judge Walker allowed police officer Don Ward to take the juror's stand and lie in his testimony, saying he served an arrest warrant upon Davis when in fact no warrant was ever served on Davis. Furthermore, as afore stated, there has never been a police report made or filed with a police officer nor any law enforcement officer.

It should be noted to the reader to the fact that there is no Statute of Limitation that would prevent the arrest of either of those above-named criminal actors.

Based on the criminal and Civil Cases that were before Judge Terrance Boyle's Court, there is no grounds to not know to the fact that Federal Court Judge Terrance Boyle lied about the unlawful conduct that were engaged by State Superior Court Judge Walker engaged regarding treasonous acts against the United States Constitution.

Walker allowed that above-named police officer to take the witness stand and lie of having served an arrest warrant upon Davis when in fact no warrant was ever served on Davis for purpose to illegally force and did force Davis into an unlawful criminal court procedure without having been designated by North Carolina Administrative Office of the Courts as expressed in Document "A." Therefore, Subject Judge Terrance W. Boyle violated federal statutory law with providing shelter for the above-named state superior court judge for interfering with the state judicial system in absence of all jurisdiction on the dates of April 13th and 14th, and it was on April 13 Davis received a shocking letter from the Assistant District Attorney ordering him to appear in the Robeson County Superior Court for a criminal trial where Davis was never charged with a crime of any type.

Why State Judge Russell G Walker should be arrested and tried in a court of Law and, when found guilty, that judge should be sentence to a federal prison.

STAGE TWO

THE BACKGROUND AND DETAIL OF FACTS THAT SHOW WHY STATE JUDGE WALKER SHOULD BE ARRESTED AND SENTENCED TO FEDERAL PRISON INCLUDING FEDERAL JUDGE TERRANCE W. BOYLE

FACTS: Judge Terrance W. Boyle very well knew that North Carolina Superior Court Judge Russell G. Walker unlawfully violated both the Constitution of North Carolina, the Law of the Land Clause, Article 19, and Violation of the laws as established under North Carolina Constitution and with Treasonous behavior with an assort upon the Constitution of the United States of American. Copies of the Criminal Complaint containing proof of a huge amount of Perjury constantly engaged by federal judge, Terrance W. Boyle in his unlawful action with documents which can be viewed by the reader Listed in Document "A."

The most important expressed Purpose of this book is to raise the conscious of the readers as the major concerns relate to a long period of thirty years of treasonous crimes against the United States Constitution and its Amendments and in total disrespect of the laws of our Nation. Further, the Purpose is to provide the awareness to the readers regarding the dangerous misuse of power that rest in the hands of those described judges. Yes, because of the seriousness of those listed crimes demand that this Author's responsibility is to enumerate each and every criminal violation against the United States Constitution and it is the responsibility of this Author to support every stated criminal treasonous conduct with authentic proof with listed attachments in a set of documents which can be viewed in Document "A." Furthermore, it is the responsibility of this Author to provide a list of witnesses, names, addresses, and telephone numbers who will or can testify under oath to the truth of the criminal claims set forth in this book—See List Of Witness attachment. As it is believed that the Federal Bureau of Investigation has been assigned to investigate those treasonous acts against the Constitution of the United States as afore mentioned. It is further the Purpose of this book to give the readers an opportunity to "Be the Judge" in regard to their observations of what will appear to be unbelievable if the specific facts were not clearly enumerated with proof, which includes a numerated list of proven Perjury. And, as to the list of Perjury, standing along is grounds for Impeachment of a state or federal judge. Therefore, the author establishes the meaning of Perjury as Codified Under Federal Statute 18 U.S. C. Code Sec. 1621, which makes it clear in saying: "Whoever having taken an oath before a competent tribunal, officer or, in any case which a law of the United States authorizes an oath to be administer, that he will testify, declare, depose, or certify truly, or that any written testimony, declaration, deposition, or certificate by him subscribed, is true, willfully and contrary to such oath states or subscribes any material matter which he does not believe to be true or in any declaration, certificate, varication, or statement under penalty of perjury as permitted under section 1746 of Title 28, United States Code, willfully subscribes as true as any material matter which he does not believe to be true; is guilty of perjury and shall, except as otherwise expressly provided by law, be find under this title or imprisoned not more than five years, or both..." Judge Terrance W. Boyle's lies were to deny Davis his Due Process Rights under the Constitution of the United States Amendments: Amendment One, Denied Free Speech to orderly express grievous in the court of law; Amendment Five, denied Davis his Rights of an Accused crime without having been charged of a crime, was never served with a warrant, denied the right to be represented by an attorney at law, and caused Davis to lose his property; Amendment Seven, Davis was denied of his Rights regarding his Civil Claims filed with both state and federal Courts; and Amendment Fourteen, Davis was denied of his guarantee Due Process Rights. Therefore, it appears that Judge Terrance W. Boyle maintained the belief that he is above the law from the standpoint that Judge Boyle never attempted to justify his treasonous acts, and nor has

Judge Boyle ever denied a single accused act against him for an assault upon the Constitution of the United States, because Judge Boyle perhaps believes that he is above the law. Furthermore, Judge Boyle has never given a response to Davis's Lawsuit file No. 7: 19-MC-6 *Robert L. Davis v. Judge Terrance W. Boyle*, which is pending before the United States District Court, Eastern District of North Carolina, of which he is required by federal stature to answer, in which the Federal Law says in regard to time of responding to a civil Complaint, "A lawsuit has been served upon you. Within 21 days after service of this summons on you (not counting the day you received it)—or 60 days if you are the United States or United States agency, or an officer or employee of the United States described in Feb. R. Civ.P.12 (a) (2) or (3)—you must serve on plaintiff an answer to the attached complaint or a motion under rule 12 of the Federal Rules of Civil Procedure. The answer or motion must be served on the plaintiff or plaintiff's attorney, whose name and address: Robert L. Davis, 40 Kensington Street, Lumberton, NC 28358."

However, it appears, Judge Boyle believed that he did not have to answer the Complaint, because that unlawful judge holds the view that he is above the law. Judge Boyle instead assigned Judge James Dever for to dismiss, and did dismiss that case in which Judge Dever did not consider any issues nor has Judge Dever ever claimed to have considered any issues set forth in that lawsuit but instead just gave the Order, dismissing the case without any word concerning a single issue. Nevertheless, that case has been reassigned to the above-named Federal District Court. Judge Boyle has not answered that Lawsuit, which was filed on May 18, 2021. According to information Davis has received from the named Federal District Court, Judge Boyle has not obtained an attorney listed with the United States Justice Department. However, Judge Boyle is fully aware of the federal law which sets the time limit of which a person must answer a lawsuit filed against him, which says: "Within 21 days after service of this summer on you (not counting the day you received it)—or 60 days if you are the United States or a United States agency, or an officer or employee of the United States described in Fed. R. Civ. P. 12 (a) (2) or (3)—you must serve on the plaintiff an answer to the attached complaint or a motion under Rule 12 of the Federal Rules of Civil Procedure as aforementioned."

Why is it that Judge Boyle has not Answered the Lawsuit filed against him with such serious charges? Davis's Answer: Perhaps Judge Terrance W. Boyle either believes he is above the law, or he has protection from a judge or judges. However, Judge Boyle knows that his actions carry not a doubt of a criminal element. Once Again, you be the Judge!

STAGE THREE

A CLOSER LOOK WITH EXAMINATION OF JUDGE TERRANCE W. BOYLE'S CRIMINAL ACTION AS TO CONSPIRACY IN CONJUNCTION WITH NORTH CAROLINA SUPERIOR COURT JUDGE RUSSELL G. WALKER

Davis has every logical reason to believe that those criminal actions engaged by Judge Boyle expressed in this book are not incidental actions but instead are occasional actions of misbehavior. However, it is important for the American citizens to know that judges under criminal behavior can and must be removed from office and placed under incarcerations.

Furthermore, the Purpose is to provide the readers a fact of Historical impeachment of Fifteen federal judges as named above. From those fifteen judges, eight were convicted. However, four of those judges were acquitted by the United States Senate, and three resigned before an outcome at trial.

We will take a brief look at the impeachment of those fifteen judges and place their unlawful conduct along aside the insurrections brought upon our nation's constitution by our current federal judge Terrance W. Boyle's insurrectionist conduct with treason against the Constitution of the United States. Following the compassion, "You Be the Judge" as to what action should be brought upon Federal Judge Terrance W. Boyle. Should the Reader, with strong conviction following the evidence, conclude that United States District Court Judge Terrance W. Boyle is a dangerous insurrectionist to our Nation's Democratic Republic? Therefore, the Reader is asked to follow at least one of the following recommended actions: a) Call your Congressional Representative; b) File a report with the Chief Judge of The

United States District Court, from which that criminal judge serves; and/or c) Report the criminal action to your Governor. In other Words, be a Champion for your Nation!

STAGE FOUR

FIRST CONSIDER THE IMPEACHMENT OF FIFTEEN FEDERAL JUDGES RANGING FROM THE YEARS OF ABOUT 1803 THROUGH 2010—BALLOTPEDIA

First, we must turn our attention to Article Three, which states that federal judges are appointed to life terms while serving "during good Behavior" (Emphasis Added) as stated in Section 1 of Article Three of the United States Constitution.

Mr. Davis requests the Reader to place a comparison of Judge Boyle's criminal conduct alongside some or all fifteen judges that were impeached.

The impeachment of federal judges in chronological order:

In the year 1804, Judge Samuel Chase of the Supreme Court of the United States was charged with Arbitrary and oppressive conduct of trials. However, Judge Chase was found to be not guilty by the United States Senate on March 1, 1805.

Comparison: On April 26, 2019, Judge Terrance W. Boyle, in Ex Parta, entered the Clerk's Office and removed Davis's lawsuit, File No. 7:19-CV-81-BO, and ordered the Clerk to inform the defendants not to answer Davis's Civil Complaint and further ordered the clerk to inform the defendants of that lawsuit to disregard the summons that were served upon them by the North Carolina, Wake County Sheriff's Department. And, as stated above, the same is listed in the Criminal Report filed with the United States Attorney General and provided with the FBI. Without a doubt, Judge Boyle's conduct was Arbitrary and Oppressive.

In the year 1830, Judge James Hawkins Peck of the United States District Court for the District of Missouri was charged with Abuse of the contempt of power. However, Judge Peck was found to be not guilty by the United States Senate in 1831.

Comparison: Judge Boyle engaged with Abuse of the Contempt of Power as it is clearly set out in this book, especially considering the seriousness of these claims against him of which Boyle has not denied none of those claims.

In the year 1862, Judge West Hughes Humphreys of the United States District Court for the Middle, Eastern, and Western Districts of Tennessee. Charges against Judge Humphreys: Refusing to hold court and waging war against the United States government, of which Judge Humphrey was convicted by the United States Senate and removed from his judgeship in the year of 1831.

Comparison: After Judge Boyle unlawfully removed Davis's Lawsuit from the Clerk's office, Judge Boyle Ordered the Clerk not to accept any matter filed with the Court by Davis. A copy of the Clerk's letter sent to Davis is included in the criminal matter assigned with the FBI. In the year of 1873, Judge Mark W. Delahey for the United States District Court for the District of Kansas was charged with haven been intoxicated while on the bench. However, Judge Delahey resigned from office before a trial in the Senate.

In the year 1904, Judge Charles Swayne United States District Court for the Northern District of Florida. Judge Swayne was charged with abuse of contempt of power and additional miss usage of office. However, judge Swayne was acquitted by the United States Senate in 1905. In the year 1913, Judge Robert Woodrow Archbold of the United States Commerce Court was charged with Improper business relation with litigants. As a result, Judge Archbold was found guilty by the United States Senate and was removed from office in 1913.

Comparison: Judge Terrance Boyle engaged illegal with those parties in Davis's Civil Action, file NO. 7:19-CV-81-BO, *Robert L. Davis v. Bryan Jr., et al.*

In the year 1918, Judge George Washington English of the United States District Court for the Eastern District of Illinois.

Judge George Washington English was charged with abuse of power. During this period in time, impeachment proceedings were dismissed.

In the year 1933, Judge Harold Louderback of the United States District for the Northern District of California. Judge Louderback was charged with favoritism in the appointment of bankruptcy. Judge Louderback was acquitted by the Senate.

In the year 1936, Judge Halsted Lockwood Ritter of the United States District Court for the Southern District of Florida. Judge Ritter was charged with Favoritism in the appointment of bankruptcy receivers and practicing law while sitting as a judge. Judge Ritter was found to be guilty by the United States Senate and was removed from office.

Comparison: Judge Terrance W. Boyle, a Federal District Court Judge and serving as an attorney at the same time for the two named Defendants in Case File No. *Robert L. Davis v. G. Bryan Collins Jr.*, 7:19-CV-81-BO

In the year of 1988, Judge Alcee Hastings of the United States District Court for the Southern District of Florida. Judge Hastings was charged with Perjury and conspiring to solicit a bribe. Judge Hasting was impeached and found guilty by the United States Senate and was removed from office in October 20, 1989.

Comparison: Judge Boyle produced a number of lies—eight actions of Perjury under the oath of his office.

In the year of 1989, Judge Walter Nixon, of the United States District Court for the Southern District of Mississippi, was charged with Perjury before a federal grand jury. Judge Walter Nixon was convicted by the United States Senate and was removed from office. Here, to be honest, Judge Boyle's eight incidents of Perjury.

Judge Samuel Kent of the United States District Court for the Southern District of Texas. Judge Samuel Kent was charged with Sexual Assault, obstructing and impending an official proceeding, and making false and misleading statements. Judge Kent resigned from office and the Article of impeachment was dismissed. Consider the false statements/Perjury made by Judge Terrance W. Boyle for the sole purpose for dismissing Davis's lawsuit—remember, Judge Boyle does not deny any claims against him. However, the controlling question: Why does Judge Terrance W. Boyle remain on the federal bench, and why do those judges who sit on the United States Appellant Court Support Judge Terrance Boyle's Treasonous acts against the Constitution of the United States when in fact all evidence was in their presence? Based on those two questions, should you be concerned about the threats against our Democracy?

And Judge Thomas Porteous of the United States District of Louisiana. Judge Thomas Porteous was charged with accepting bribes and making false statements under penalty. Judge Thomas Porteous was convicted by the Senate and was removed from office in 1994.

Comparison: The four hundred dollars Judge Boyle had withdrawn from the United States Treasurer and presented to Davis appears to have been a bribe to keep Davis quiet with respect of Boyle's unlawful conduct. Judge Boyle should or should have known that the court does not reward funds back to a defendant even if he thought the defendant's Complaint were baseless.

A THROUGH LOOK WITH COMPARISONS OF FEDERAL JUDGE TERRANCE BOYLE'S CRIMINAL CONDUCT IN COMPARISON WITH THOSE IMPEACHED JUDGES

First, Judge Terrance W. Boyle's Conspiracy in conjunction with the criminal conduct of two above-named State Superior Court Judges, Russell G. Walker and G. Bryan Collins, in relation to his abuse and treasonous acts against both the Constitution of North Carolina and the United States Constitution and its Amendments.

FACTS:

Again, one of the most outstanding Purposes of this book is to rattle the minds of the readers to become fully aware of the true facts that a growing threat is on the rise against our nation's democratic governmental institutions as to the treasonous acts by the name judge in this book, along with such avocation of "Stop The Steal Vote," and other growing bitter groups could very well lead to a Coup d e'tat movement, and by the same token, a federal judge such as described in this book is waging treasonous acts against the Constitution of the United States, and little or no actions are been taking by the state or federal Appellant Courts, of which these courts either turn a blind eye or circumvent many criminal acts that are brought fourth, such as complaints filed by way of lawsuits and complaints filed with judicial Commissions on both state and federal levels. However, the United States have very great confirmed Judges on the bench and very good citizens who serve in political office. Many citizens who are leaders in their communities who love and cherish our Nation's democratic institutions and are impressed to the degree that they will become advocates to friends and foe not to take the American Democratic institutions for granted, but instead report any matter or persons who appear to be a danger to our national democratic institutions such as discussed in pages above as related to the criminal conduct of Judge Terrance W. Boyle and supported by those federal judges who had those Treasonous actions before them.

In recounting the history of the thirty years of insurrections by the identified criminal actions regarding the subject judge named brings to the attention regarding January 6, 2021, the insurrection that rained upon our nation's capital. Therefore, the most important purpose for writing this book is to give the readers a clear destination regarding the insurrection brought upon the Capital of the United States and the insurrection waged upon the Constitution of the United States by way of treasonous acts resulting from criminal conspiracy in conjunction with federal Judge Boyle and with state judges.

Just from the viewpoint of haven watched the insurrection on television, such action may appear for more dangerous than that of those unlawful concerned judges. However, the vast difference is to the fact, among the thousands who participated in the January 6 Insurrection, perhaps had no high school diploma, no college degree, and perhaps were even unemployed or, unfortunately, just had a need for affiliation. Nevertheless, these judges such as Judge Boyle and those judges who disregard the criminal actions committed by Judge Boyle are well educated, highly paid, and appointed federal judges and with unlimited time on the bench. However, judges are not free to engage criminal conduct such as described by the author of the named judge herein.

The President of the United States very carefully appoints well-qualified persons to be placed before the United States Senate for confirmation hearings, of which the Senate confirms the nominees to be placed on the Judiciary Branch to sit on the bench for the entire purpose to protect the rights granted under the United States Constitution and provide the American Public a free and just means to bring grievous matters to the court for protection of their rights, which were provided by our nation's fathers in the formation of the

Nation's Constitution in the year 1787, which strongly stands during our time and respected around the world in every international community.

The purpose is to adjust the readers' viewpoint from seeing the insurrection from a television set, such as the January 6 insurrection, which appeared to be more dangerous against our democratic institutions than the unlawful conduct of our nation's few judges committed in a joint conspiracy such as has been active by Judge Terrance W. Boyle. However, it is to the contrary based on the mere fact that the severe treasonous acts, neglect of the federal judge's legal and statutory duty, malfeasance, misfeasance, and nonfeasance of the named judge herein. Therefore, should the reader look at the insurrection engaged by corrupt federal judges through a microscope, it will certainly reveal that those treasonous acts are committed in secrecy, of which no one can see on television nor read in the newspaper. However, those named concerned judges in no way represent the vast majority of our Nation's outstanding characteristics of our State and Federal Judges who serve and lead our Judiciary Branch of Government here in the United States of America.

Well, may it be said by the reader, "why trouble yourself just because of those few judges who engaged those unlawful acts set out in this book? Doesn't mean that those few judges are a threat to our Nation!" If that statement were to be made, it would be very important that the reader consider two factors: First, as related to the French Revolution, where many people were disgusted with living under a Monarchy dictatorship, of which a few disgusted people met on the Tennis Court in Versailles on June 20, 1789, and took an oath which resorted to their success with the overthrow of the Monarchy in 1799, which was headed by King Louis XVI who met his death along with his wife, Marie Antoinette, at the Guillotine, and from that few grew to the point where centuries of dictatorship under a Monarchy were brought to an end. Therefore, never rule out the danger of the few who present a danger to our nation's democracy, and Second, be mindful of the United States Title 18 U.S.C. Section 2382, which says: "Whoever, owing allegiance to the United States and having knowledge of the commission of treason against them, conceals and does not, as soon as may be, disclose and make known the same to the President or to some judge of the United States, or to the governor or to some justice of a particular state, is guilty of misprision of treason and shall be fined under this title or imprisoned not more than seven years, or both." Clearly, this is the purpose for writing this book is related to corrupt judges. Moreover, the Author, a victim, of the criminal actions engaged by the subject judge listed in this book followed the proper procedures as related to the matter of reporting criminal and corrupt activities by both state and federal judges. The procedures of which Davis employed consist as follows: 1) Gained a clear, unmistakable fact that a judge has engaged treasonous acts against the Amendments and the Constitution of the United States; 2) Maintained all material documents of proof; 3) Maintained names of persons who could be witnesses, telephone numbers, email addresses, and physical addresses; and 4) Should, for example, criminal treasonous acts neglect of the judge's legal and statutory duty malfeasance, misfeasance, and nonfeasance who you, with complete knowledge, has violated the United States Constitution and its Amendments, and has conspired with others to violate the US Constitution, and where a judge uses his or her powerful station to unlawfully by order forced any employee(s) to engage in any felonious crimes against the principles of the United States Constitution and its Amendments such as was done by Judge Terrance W. Boyle as is revealed. Yes, Report Those Dangerous Judges to The Proper Authorities without delay.

However, let's be clear, those handful of judges in no way represent the commitment of the many men and women who serve our judicial system; and 5) File a well-prepared criminal report with at least one of the following: a) a Chief Judge of the Federal Jurisdiction where the Criminal Judge is assigned; b) the President of The United States; c) The United States Justice Department; d) The governor of your state; and e) Be careful not to discuss those matters with other people who hold no authority to provide corrections or punishment relating to the treasonous conduct of a judge. However, never attempt to take any matter into one's own hands. Further, should one find that he or she is a victim of such criminal action by a state or federal judge, Davis would strongly suggest such person consult with an attorney. The chief purpose for this suggestion is to the fact that a presiding or ruling judge in a civil case, for example, might give a verdict which may not at all aligned with the law, in which one filed in a court or charged with a crime that may carry serious consequences. PLEASE CONSULT an attorney! Nonetheless, it maybe said, IT IS NONE OF DAVIS'S BUSINESS HOW ONE DEALS WITH HIS or HER AFFAIRS. Davis would just say, "Just Suggesting."

Therefore, in support of the Authenticity of this book, case law has been listed herein and filed documented cases with the court; file case numbers also appear in this book. Furthermore, in support of the truth as to the listed criminal action cited as committed by any named judge, federal statutes, and the Amendments to the United States Constitution are listed along with facts regarding judges who were impeached as previous stated and who committed similar crimes such as the subject judge named in this book. Therefore, the following Judges who were impeached and the charges upon which those judges were placed before the Honorable United States House of Representatives and the United States Senate—for trial and conviction in the following Chronological Order:

STAGE FIVE

A BRIEF BACKGROUND OF THE JUDGE'S FELONIOUS CRIMINAL ACTIONS FIRST BEGINNING WITH NC STATE JUDGE RUSSELL G. WAKER

On the evening of March 19, 1992, in the City of Lumberton, North Carolina, Robert L. Davis (Herein After Referred to as "Davis") had returned home at approximately 5:20 p.m. from the Fairmont High School, where he taught history and civics. While at home, Davis did what he normally would after dinner, which was enter his study room, which he normally used for his school preparation as well as for his church business. On that concerned evening, Davis was sitting in his home office grading papers from the work of his students, which had been completed from a quiz during the last fifteen minutes of his class that day. However, during the hour of about 9:05 p.m., Davis's second-grade son heard a knock on the front door of the home. The son noticed the presence of two uniformed police officers from the Lumberton Police Department. From where Davis was located in his office, he could not detect that a knock was ever made at the front door of their home; otherwise, Davis would have gone to the door himself because of the time during which the knock occurred. Nevertheless, Davis's son came and knocked on his office door and said, "Dad, there are two policemen at the door."

Davis immediately went to the front door, and truly, there stood two uniformed Lumberton police officers who asked, "Are you, Robert Davis?"

Davis answered, "Yes I am." At this junction, the senior officer identified himself as Sergeant Mark Bradly, and Officer Bradly identified the younger person as Officer Don Ward, also with the Lumberton Police Department. of whom was under Sergeant Bradly's supervision. During which time Davis was before those two police officers, the younger officer Ward never said one word. However, Senior Officer Mark Bradly did all of the speaking. Senior Officer Bradly said, "Sir, we are here to arrest you on a crime that you committed a little earlier today."

Davis then asked the officers, "For what purpose?"

Senior Officer Bradly said, "Sir, we do not want to discuss this in front of your young son, and you can drive your own vehicle to the police station a few minutes after we leave your property, of which your neighbors will not think nothing about anything and where we can talk about this."

Davis asked the police officers, "About what?" The two policemen uniformly turned their faces directly staring toward each other, making no comments, which appeared to have lasted for about six seconds at this point. Davis asked the senior officer, "Do you have an arrest warrant for my arrest?"

Officer Bradly answered with what appeared to have been an anger in his voice, "No!" Immediately the officer's voice dropped very low, "I have no arrest warrant. This is about a crime of indecent exposure that you committed, sir." Officer Bradly continued to say, "Sir, you can come to the police station in your own vehicle, or we can take you the hard way, which would not be a good sight for your young son and family."

The officer allowed Davis to speak to his wife and dress for the trip down to the Lumberton Police Station. Davis's wife, Betty, then asked him, "When and where did the police say that happened?"

Davis then told his wife, "I am going down to the police station to see what he"—Officer Bradly—"is talking about."

Betty asked Davis, "Did the police name a place?"

Davis answered quickly, "No, no, he did not say. I got to go!" Davis was somewhat apprehensive, with a thought in mind that those officers would return and use force to take him in one of their police cars. Davis did not want either to be the case in his community. At about 9:47 p.m., Davis met the two police officers at the police station in a large room of what appeared to be a conference room for dignitaries where Davis was invited to sit with the two officers at a large table with water and drinks sitting on the table. Both officers appeared to be in a very friendly mood. The senior officer asked Davis to have a seat and asked, "How does your day go?"

Davis, with apprehension, said "Very well."

Officer Bradly was, at this point, ready to go into the arrest conversation. Officer Bradly asked Junior Officer Don Ward, "Do you want to take it from here?"

Officer Don Ward said, "I'll pass; you can do it."

At this point, Officer Bradly then proceeded to tell Davis that he had been in the "Biggs Parks Shopping parking lot" and further stated that "a number of witnesses called in reporting that you were exposing yourself in the parking lot, and someone made a call reporting the indecent act you committed." Davis, at that point, asked the officer once again to produce an arrest warrant. Officer Bradly insisted that an arrest warrant was not required and that he did not have a warrant. However, Officer Bradly Told Davis that he would have a date set for trial in the Robeson County District Court in about three weeks, and it will all come out then. At this point, Davis stated that he needed to see a written warrant and what crime he was charged with and those people who claimed that he committed a crime. When Davis told the officers that he wanted to know who were some of those people who claimed to have seen him exposing himself in the Biggs Parking Lot. Officer Bradly stated, "Sir, like I said, you will know all of that in about three weeks, maybe four. It will all come out in the courtroom before a judge."

Two high-ranking persons with the Lumberton Police Department provided information completely in opposite of that which Officer Bradly said regarding "a number of witnesses called in reporting that you were exposing yourself." Chief of Police Harry Dolan and Captain Johnson stated there were absolutely no phone calls made by anyone regarding any matter of indecent exposure. However, Davis did not stop there; he went to the dispatcher with the question as to any calls that might have been made to the Lumberton Police Department on the evening of March 19, 1992, between the time of 6:00 p.m. and 7:00 p.m. The Dispatcher shook her head, saying, "No such calls were ever made."

When Davis arrived home, he was in high spirits even though it was about twelve midnight. His wife, Betty, was still up. Davis related to his wife, saying,

"It really won't amount to anything because those officers did not even know how to lie straight." Davis and his wife turned in for that morning around 1:30 a.m. Davis got up early that morning on the 20th of March 1992 on his way to his high school with a mindset that gave him a strong feeling that such a bogus claim was less than a cake walk. On March 23, 1992, Davis obtained an attorney, John W. Campbell, whose office was stationed in Lumberton, and the attorney was associated with a renowned name as a criminal trial lawyer whose office was "Clearly" located in the inner parts of the city of Lumberton. At 8:30 a.m., Davis entered Attorney Campbell's office as was scheduled. Attorney John W. Campbell asked Davis if he brought a copy of the arrest warrant. Davis informed Attorney Campbell that the arresting officer did not serve an arrest warrant upon him. Attorney Campbell told Davis that the officers had to have served an arrest warrant upon him. Based upon the expression on Attorney Campbell's face, it appeared to the fact that the attorney may have believed Davis may not have been truthful in saying the officers did not serve an arrest warrant up on him. Therefore, Davis decided to tell his attorney that the officers may have filed the arrest warrant in the clerk's office (Referring to the Court Clerk). At that moment, Attorney Britt told Davis to come back to his office on Thursday, March 26, and he would discuss the case and fee. So, on March 26 at 8:30 a.m., Davis met with his Attorney, Mr. Campbell, at which time Mr. Campbell informed Davis to the fact that the police officers did not serve an arrest warrant at all. Davis then asked Mr. Campbell if it were possible for him to gain any information as to who were the people who supposedly called in a crime of indecent exposure. At that time, Attorney Campbell said, "Let's take one step at a time, and that step involves the fee, if you are willing to go forward with this, of which you should be considering your status as a schoolteacher and preacher."

Davis replied, "Go for it, Mr. Attorney," Mr. Campbell set his legal fee at fifteen hundred dollars. Mr. Campbell said that he realized that the price for legal service was quite excessive for a misdemeanor.

Without Davis saying a word, Attorney Campbell made a statement of explanation, "Even though it's a misdemeanor, I will be fighting to save your reputation as a minister and a teacher, so it is worth that and more." Davis obtained Attorney Campbell to represent him in that criminal matter.

Davis returned to Attorney Campbell's office on Monday, the 29th as scheduled at 8:30 a.m. After waiting outside of Mr. Campbell's office, which appeared to have been his secretary's office, Mr. Campbell comes out of his office very slowly and says to Davis, "What I have found out is not good news for us." Then Mr. Campbell speaks up with a quick voice, "Come on in!" Then Mr. Campbell says, "We don't need to talk in front of that gal out there"—referring to his secretary. "Have a seat." Mr. Campbell went on to tell Davis that a well-known banker who works for Southern National Bank and Trust Company will place his teenage daughter on the witness stand and declare that you exposed yourself in her direction. Mr. Campbell went on to say that it will be a hard battle to fight, and Mr. Campbell advised Davis, "The banker will claim that you confessed to them at the police station, saying you said, 'I did it.'" With that statement, Davis did not know who the "them" were because no one met at the police station but Davis and the two officers who had come to his house on the evening of the 19th. At that point, Mr. Campbell asked Davis if he had the money order for his legal fee. Previously, Mr. Campbell had not said anything about a money order. Even though Davis had his bank check book, Davis did not mention to Attorney Campbell that he had his check book. Instead, Davis told Attorney that he would let him know something later during the day. However, Davis did not get back with Mr. Campbell at all during that day. Instead, when Davis's wife, Betty, returned home from her school and their children were at their school working with their instrument teacher, Davis and his wife Betty went to the nearby City in Dillion, South Carolina, for dinner, where Davis went over the message of which Attorney Campbell told him. However, because of Attorney Campbell's reputation in the community, Davis and his wife Betty agreed to pay the legal fee in the amount of fifteen hundred dollars, considering Davis's reputation needed to be protected. However, a person whom Davis knew who worked in some capacity at Southern National Bank and Trust Company informed Davis that a high-ranking person named Phillip Floyd, who headed the Trustee Department and was known to have lived in Davis's neighborhood, about three houses just north of Davis's house, and was father of the teenage girl whom Attorney Campbell spoke was expected to be placed before the court to testify against Davis. For the first time, Davis become fully aware that his sincere trouble surely had arrived. The thought "cake walk" disappeared from Davis's mind.

On May 27, 1992, at 11:00 a.m., Davis with his Attorney John W. Campbell took their seats on the left side of the Robeson County District Court in the city of Lumberton with a very young judge, James Carmichael, who would preside in that criminal matter as neither of the Senior level District Court Judges wanted to handle that case and therefore pushed the matter off on the younger judge, Carmichael, as Davis was informed. The banker's fifteen-year daughter, Jamie Michell Floyd, was seated on the right next to the state prosecuting attorney. Davis entered a plea of "not guilty." As Davis sat beside his attorney, Davis was whispering to his attorney to make a motion for dismissal on grounds that he was never arrested nor was an arrest warrant ever served upon him. However, Davis's Attorney, Mr. Campbell, whispered a question to Davis, "What for?"

Davis answered, "For lack of evidence, and it was a warrantless arrest, and no charge was made against me. You know that, Mr. Attorney!"

Finally, Mr. Campbell said, "I won't do it. Just let me do my job, Mr. Davis. I want to help you." At that moment, Davis knew he was in serious trouble.

The young girl, Jamie Floyd, took the stand and appeared to be very uncomfortable. She spoke in a voice that barely could be heard. When Davis's attorney asked Jamie Floyd the question, "When did you report the incident?" Jamie Floyd answered, "After it happened."

The attorney, "And who did you report that to?"

Jamie Floyd answered, "I reported it to my dad and mom. They were inside the store."

Attorney Britt, "Do you reckon what time it was?"

Jamie Floyd, "It was six something o'clock." Jamie Floyd released her first lie before the court on the basic fact that Jamie Floyd's Mother, Frankie, and Father were separated, and her Father Phillip was living with another woman in the nearby town of Fairmount, of whom Phillip Floyd married a short time thereafter, perhaps less than a year. At this junction, the young Judge under heavy pressure rendered a judgement: "guilty." The judge gave Davis a ninety-day sentence, suspension, and a fifty-dollar fine.

Immediately following, Attorney Campbell said to Davis, "I still think that you are innocent, but this was a tough case." The first thing that struck Davis's mind was the belief his attorney was a participator with the accusers. Attorney Britt further stated, "With a fee of five thousand dollars, we can appeal this damn thing." Davis shot back with anger at the Attorney with a Snap, "No way!"

Davis joined his Wife Betty and left the courtroom. Davis did not pay the fifty-dollar fine imposed by the court because he timely appealed the court's ruling to the Superior Court of Robeson County, North Carolina.

On the date of February 12, 1993, Davis drove to the United States Post Office to check his Post Office Box as normal, but instead came in contact with a friend minister who had served in the North Carolina General Assembly, the House of Representatives, along with a well-known Lawyer whom Davis's friend minister recommended that he contact that attorney. A few days later, Davis drove from Lumberton to Raleigh and met with that Attorney, who agreed to take Davis's Case.

On April 13, 1993, Davis heard what appeared to be the mail carrier's vehicle nearing his area as the mail was delivered each day. Nevertheless, the strange fact about that day, the sound Davis heard was indeed the mailman on his normal mail route. However, that time of the delivery of mail was not normal at all. It was 8:42 a.m., and the usual time for the mail delivery on Davis's residential street each day was between the hours of 3:40 to 4:20 p.m. (During the period of the '90s). Whatever that time of delivery meant, Davis will perhaps never know. One thing Davis came on to learn was the fact that he received a letter in his mailbox from the state Prosecutor's office ordering him to be in the superior court the very next day, April 14, 1993, at 10:00 a.m. for his criminal trial, which was set to be tried by a jury. Certainly, Davis was very frightened because he had absolutely no time to contact his expected lawyer. However, at about 1:00 p.m., Davis filed a handwritten motion for discovery in the court for purpose to see whatever he was charged with and whom he would face in the superior court and what would be brought before the court against him—a copy of the same is listed with this book—See Document "A." Another strange observation about the state prosecutor's notice to Davis to appear in court was the fact that letter was dated April 12th, and Davis received the letter on April 13th, and he was to be in court for his criminal trial the very next day, April 14. Anyway, Davis became very frightened for several reasons: he had very little time, if any, to contact his lawyer who agreed to handle his criminal case. Davis became even more frightened after several unsuccessful attempts to reach the attorney by phone, and the person who answered Davis's phone call informed Davis that the lawyer was in a committee meeting, of which that lawyer was the chairman of that committee and he could not leave out of that committee meeting. A spell of emotion came upon Davis when the hour of 5:00 p.m. had passed on the day of the 13th. Within about twenty minutes, Davis's nerves began to settle down as he began to convince himself that all he had to do was ask the presiding judge to postpone the trial until he contacted his lawyer. Davis, as a history and civic teacher, extended his thinking with the thought, "After all, the United States Constitution will not allow a court to try anyone without council in the court of law and where no arrest warrant was issued." Davis spoke out verbally to himself, "That's it, I got it, yes!"

On the very next day, April 14, 1993, Davis was before the Superior Court of Robeson County on appeal de novo for his trial. An assistant clerk met Davis just as he entered the courthouse and informed him that a judge (Walker) had denied his motion for discovery written on the same paper of his hand written Motion. Davis entered the courtroom at 9:59 a.m., according to his watch, where he sat until 11:12 a.m., and at which time the clerk called the Case Number 92 CRS 0065 *State vs. Robert Lee Davis*. The Judge, Russell Walker, called for Robert Davis to step up and have a seat on the left side, while the state prosecutor, Mr. Stan Todd, took his seat along with the banker's fifteen-year-old daughter, Jamie Floyd, seated on the right side of the courtroom closer to the jury. That was frightening enough to Davis. At the very beginning of the court trail session, Davis raised his hand, at which time Judge Russell Walker asked, "What is it, Mr. Davis?"

Davis answered, "I am asking that this trial be postponed until I get in touch with my lawyer whose office is located in Durham. I just received my letter from the state yesterday to be here in court today."

At that point, Judge Walker holds up his hand with his palm facing Davis saying, "Stop! Your motion is denied. I have the understanding that you, Mr.

Davis, are capable of handling your own criminal trial." Davis became even more confused as to where did Judge Walker got such information about him handling his own matter in court. However, the trial proceeded, with Davis choosing the jury along with the well-experienced state prosecutor that would try his case. Here, Davis had a strange feeling on two fronts: First, there was no oath given by the court to the jury as required, and second, the official thought of choosing the jury against a well-experienced state's assistant prosecutor such as that of Stan Todd rather than one of the weakest assistants in electing his jury. However, the jury was selected, and the trial got underway, with Davis having absolutely no experience whatsoever in trying a case at his own criminal trial, especially considering the removal of his teaching career resulting from this concerning allegation and the losing of his pastoral position and the embarrassment brought upon his family. However, to be clear, Davis decided upon his own to resign from his church for what he thought was best for the church, even though Davis was encouraged not to resign but did so anyway, thinking it was best for the church because of the church's outstanding name.

At the close of the arguments by first the state prosecutor, followed by Davis, it was now time for the judge to charge the Jury. During the charging of the Jury, Judge Russell Walker committed a terrible crime by presenting the false incriminating evidence before the jury, saying: "Ladies and gentlemen, the Court has ruled that in the instance of this case, under all the evidence, Mr. Davis voluntarily went with the officers to the police department and there from went voluntarily to the Magistrate's office to appear before the Magistrate; under those circumstances no arrest was made and no arrest warrant was required under the law of the State of North Carolina." Portion of the Court Transcript is listed in this book.

The Jury's rendered a verdict of "guilty."

At this point as to Providing protection for State Judge Walker as to Perjury: 1. Judge Boyle Stated in his Order in Case File Number *Davis v. Walker*, 7:98-CV-116, where Judge Boyle declared under oath With Perjury saying that he entertained all issues in that case. Give Notice to the Following: a) Nothing was mentioned regarding Davis was denied discovery; b) Nothing was mentioned regarding Davis having been brought to a criminal trial without having been charged with a crime and Davis was brought to trial without a warrant ever served upon him; c) Davis was denied to have his attorney to represent him in a criminal court trial; d) Nothing was mentioned regarding the incriminating statements made to the jury by State Court Judge Walker; d) Nothing was mentioned regarding the perjury Judge Walker allowed, which was a young teenage girl, Jamie Floyd, and her Father, Phillip Floyd, to testify with perjury to the jury; and e) nothing was said regarding Judge Boyle's Order as to Davis's illegal imprisonment, illegal resulting from the corrupt criminal trial court probation, and illegal five-hundred-dollar fine. By belief and information, Davis was informed by a high-ranking person from the clerk's office that the five hundred dollars was given to Jamie Floyd as a gift to purchase her material for tennis sport.

Approximately, in the year of 2001, later in the evening, Assistant District Attorney Stan Tod came over to Davis's truck and talked with Davis for about thirty or forty seconds, at which time Mr. Todd asked Davis to forgive him for prosecuting him under such unlawful matter. Davis felt the sincerity in Mr. Todd's voice until water started streaming from Davis's eyes to the point where Davis did not want to enter the post office with water coming down from his eyes, especially when there appeared to be no stopping of the tears; Davis slowly got back in his truck with the thought in mind, "I'll check my mail tomorrow."

STAGE SIX

NORTH CAROLINA STATE SUPERIOR COURT JUDGE RUSSELL G. WALKER'S TREASONOUS ACTS AGAINST STATE AND FEDERAL CONSTITUTIONS

Insurrectionist Judge Russell Walker, at all times, served the State of North Carolina from a different Judicial DISTRICT 19, and as stated under North Carolina State Statutory Law, a judge cannot preside in any other district within the state without the assignment of North Carolina Administrative Officer of the Courts, which is an arm to North Carolina Supreme Court. Therefore, where judge Russell Walker assigned himself to preside in the Robeson County Superior Court, which is a different Judicial District 16, Judge Walker acted outside of his jurisdiction and therefore become a law violator, and where a judge is lawfully assigned in a different judicial district, a certificate is provided with the County Court Clerk. However, as to the matter involving Judge Russell Walker serving on a Judicial District, he unlawfully engaged treasonous acts, neglect of his legal and statutory duty, malfeasance, and nonfeasance and conspired with others to wage an attack upon the Constitution of North Carolina, Article I, Sections 19, 20, 21, 23, and the Constitution of the United States. The United States Supreme Court had ruled several times holding that any judge who acts without jurisdiction is engaged in an act of treason: *US vs, Will*, 449 U.S. 200, 216, 101 S. Ct. 471, 66 L.Ed. 2d 392, 406 (1980); *Chens v. Virginia*, 19 U.S. (6 Weat) 264, 404. 5 LED 257 (1821}.

The United States Supreme Court went to say engaging in an act of treason against the United States Constitution by any citizen of the United States is an act of war against the United States: *Cooper v. Aaron*, 358 U.S. U.S. 1, 78 S. 78 S. Ct.1401 (1958).

Under the law of the United States, Due process is a requirement of the United States Constitution. Violation of the United States Constitution by a judge deprives that person from being a judge under the law. Therefore, when a judge violates the Constitution of the United States, it deprives that person from bring a judge under the law. Thus, that judge will be acting only as a private citizen. Therefore, no private citizen has the right to preside over matters in the court of law.

The question could be raised: Was Judge Russel Walker paid to benefit certain persons, or does it matter whether Walker was paid or not? Judge Walker was not a judge at all in handling Davis Criminal Trial. The Question may be raised, Did Judge Walker take a bribe to unlawfully engage in the criminal act as he engaged and where such action was under criminal conduct of taking a bribe, which is an impeachment offence, where the judge engaged insurrection against North Carolina Statutes, State Constitution, the federal Statutes, and the Constitution of the United States?

Now, at this juncture, the reader may very well raise the question, How was Judge Walker able to escape with such crimes? Davis would suggest that based on the grounds that the Judge did get away should demand every citizens' mind to become concerned to the fact that Our Nation's Democracy is certainly in severe danger.

Here, Judge Walker set the stage for the incoming federal judges named herein to demonstrate their unlawful conduct with Treason and Imprisonment against the United States Constitution. The frightening question that came to Davis's mind, "Does this creep represent a democratic society?" Davis further thought about a period a few years back when he was in the Soviet Union and how proud he was of having a citizenship in Good Old USA. Yes, Davis leads himself to question, "Is our Democratic Government under threat, resulting from actions of lifetime appointed judges similar to that of Judge Terrance W. Boyle?" May Davis say to the reader of this book, it would be very difficult to find one who is willing to file a complaint against a federal judge. This person, Davis, is in a miserable position of having to file a complaint against Judge Terrance W. Boyle. However, Davis's sense of reasonability as a citizen outweighs his miserable taste of filing a criminal complaint against criminal actions engaged by federal judges.

Now, back to Jamie Floyd: It must be clearly understood the young Girl, Jamie Floyd, did not have a single person as a witness on her behalf despite the lies that were told claiming many phone calls were made to the police department. However, there was at least ONE ILLEGAL WITNESS ON BEHALF OF JAMIE FLOYD: That person was the unlawful presiding Judge without jurisdiction, Russel G. Walker, following the closing arguments of Prosecutor Todd and Defendant Davis.

Judge Russell Walker did as any other judge instructed the Jury concerning reaching a verdict. However, after the instruction to the Jury, Judge Walker lied (Committed Perjury) to the Jury under incriminating statements, saying, as stated preciously, Davis confessed at the police station and therefrom Davis voluntarily went to the magistrate's office and confessed of having committed a crime of indecent exposure. Davis has absolutely no idea where that illegal judge got such false information.

Furthermore, Judge Walker was well aware of the crime of perjury where the named illegal state judge allowed the young girl, Jamie M. Floyd, to commit such perjury under oath in the jury box saying she became so sick, claiming that she went to a doctor and a Psychiatrist and further saying she missed a lot of days out of school, falsely claiming her absence from school was as a resort of the false alleged indecent exposure.

Based on the fact Davis was denied discovery, following that trial, Davis visited the Lumberton High School Principal and obtained a copy of the young girl Jamie Floyd's attendance records, which revealed the true fact that Jamie Floyd did not miss a single day out of school from the 18th day of March through the remaining of the '91–92 school year. A copy of the aforementioned girl's attendance record is added to this book–See Document "A." Judge Walker's criminal words to the jury were made as a reason to justify a warrantless arrest. Not a single person provided such testimony as was stated by Judge Walker before the jury. Therefore, Judge Walker committed a crime of Perjury under the color of his office. In spite of the fact, Judge Walker is not above the law, no action has been taken against that judge's unlawful criminal action in absence of all jurisdictions with an assort upon both the State of North Carolina and the United States Constitutions as to Davis's knowledge.

Another criminal act presented to the jury where Judge Walker enjoined himself with a Police Officer, Don Ward, who brought forth a Magistrate Order unknown to Davis as a means to justify a warrantless arrest which caused Davis's Court trial. The Magistrate Order contained no one's name as to making a complaint; Robert Davis's name was not on the Magistrate Order. A 32 Kensington Street was listed at the top of the said Order, which was not Davis's address, nor the Address of Jamie Floyd and no name was listed in. The Magistrate's Order specifically stated that a crime had been committed. In other words, the Magistrate's Order was a calculated fraud with percussion to engaged the treasonous acts, neglect of his legal and statutory duty, malfeasance, and nonfeasance, of North Carolina State Judge Russell Walker and Federal Judge Terrance W. Boyle in a calculated conspiracy who have violated the United States Constitution, specifically: the First Amendment protects the citizens to petition the government for redress of grievances; Amendment Four prohibits forcing a person to a criminal court without an arrest warrant and therefore no probable cause; Amendment Five requires that no person be denied of life, liberty, or property without due process of law; Amendment Six requires that a person be ascertained by law and to be informed of the nature and cause of the accusation; the Seventh Amendment requires that a person tried before a just jury; and the Fourteenth Amendment says in pennant parts: "No state shall make or enforce any law which shall abridge the privileges or immunities of citizens of the United States; nor shall any state deprive any person of life, liberty, or property, without due process of law; nor deny to any person within its jurisdiction the equal protection of the laws." Therefore, Judge Walker and Judge Boyle, in a joint conspiracy, engaged in acts of corruptions and have engaged in the crime of defrauding the United States government.

FACT: Judges Russell Walker and Terrance Boyle are Not Above the Law.

Judge Walker not only engaged perjury but knowingly allowed the fifteen-year-old girl Jamie Floyd's Father Phillip Floyd and to testify under oath at trial falsely. First, Phillip Floyd's act of Perjury saying, as the state Prosecutor asked Phillip Floyd, "What effect has this had on your daughter, as far as you can see?" Phillip Floyd's Answer: "My daughter chooses to appear very strong on this issue, but we kept her out of school; she refused to go to school several days. She had stomach troubles. She couldn't stand up straight. We had her visit Doctor Robert Young for this condition. He prescribed some medicines that were similar to a Tagamet, something to ease the stress, and she would stay home for a day at a time..." That statement was a lie—perjury under oath in the jury witness seat. What action was ever taken against Phillip Floyd? ANSWER: NONE! Question to you the Reader, "Does such action represent Democracy?" However, while Jamie Floyd lied under oath, she never testified as to the above testimony given by her father, Phillip Floyd.

Accordingly, Jamie Floyd's 1991–92 School Year Attendance Record, as above stated, shows the true fact of Phillip Floyd's lies regarding Janie Floyd's absence from school. Accordingly, During the school year 1991–92, Jamie Floyd missed fourteen days that school year, of which Jamie Floyd did not miss a single day out of school from March 18th through the remaining days of that school year, of which June 5, 1992, was the last school day. Therefore, Judge engaged in a conspiracy with Phillip and Jamie Floyd's lies as means to criminally engage treasonous acts, neglect of his legal and statutory duty malfeasance, misfeasance, and nonfeasance with violation of North Carolina Constitution, Article 19, the United States Constitution and its Amendments. Therefore, Judge Russell Walker engaged in acts of corruption and has engaged in the felonious crimes of defrauding the Constitutions of North Carolina and the Constitution of the United States.

Judge Walker knew or should have known that North Carolina General statute 1A1, Rule 26, North Carolina Rules of Civil Procedures, provided Davis the right of discovery.

However, the court trial record will show that Davis argued strenuously at trial that a warrant was never served upon him at any time. Furthermore, state witness Jami Floyd testified that she nor her parents filed a complaint against Davis. Based on Jamie's testimony, Davis was relying with confidence based on the fundamental fairness concept of both the State and Federal Constitutions. North Carolina Constitutional precepts that the peoples should be secure in their person, as stated in North Carolina Constitution Article 1, Section 22. Moreover, Presiding Judge Russell Walker knew that North Carolina Constitution was to protect Davis against the abuses of arbitrary arrest. Regarding the matter of arrest without a warrant except as authorized by statute is illegal. A major case related to Davis's matter was ruled upon in 1954, in the case *State v. Mobley*, 240 N.C. 476, 83 S.E. 2d 100 (1954). Judge Russell Walker's criminal action appears to have premedicated to the degree, which drove him from his judicial district illegally with the objective to place a verdict of guilty upon Davis. Furthermore, Judge Walker engaged a serious criminal act knowingly in the violation of Davis's rights protected under the United States Constitution Amendment Four and North Carolina General Statute lSA-401, which requires the officers to obtain a warrant before making an arrest, of which an arrest was never made upon Davis.

Judge Walker committed a crime based on the fact of allowing Police Officer Don Ward to lie before the court during the time that officer was in the witness seat under cross-examination. When Davis asked Officer Ward if he did issue an arrest Warrant, Officer Ward answered "Yes." Officer Ward went on to say that he issued an arrest warrant upon Davis and further stated that he could not have arrested Davis should he not have a warrant for Davis's arrest. However, in just seconds, Officer Ward changed his testimony later in the cross-examination stage. Officer Ward stated saying that the magistrate issued a magistrate's order on Davis was a lie. At this point, Judge Walker was in full knowledge that no document of any kind was listed in the court record as an arrest warrant or magistrate's order while Police Officer Ward was engaging perjury under oath regarding both Federal and State law. Federal law, which is entitled "False declaration before grand jury or court." Therefore, Judge Walker was in criminal error for not giving instruction at that point, especially where Officer Ward engaged perjury as to both state and federal law. Federal law, which is entitled "False declaration before grand jury or court." 18 U.S.C. Section 1623, State Law General Statute 14-209. Judge Walker's crime came by way of failing to give instruction during the perjurious testimonies of Officer Ward.

The Jury returned with a verdict of "GUILTY!"

APPEALS TAKEN TO THE NORTH CAROLINA COURT OF APPEALS

Upon the jury's guilty verdict, Davis was of the belief that his Appeal to the North Carolina Court of Appeals would set him free while making a list of factors which the Walker's court had unlawfully engaged. Therefore, Davis made a list of favorable issues that surely would set him free with the thought driving through his mind, "This appeal involves a substantial question of Federal and state Constitutional Law"; based on the fact, among which included First, the allegation was said to have taken place in a public parking lot, Biggs Park Parking Lot, of which provided no specific location in the Biggs parking lot, which was the largest parking lot in Robeson County and the fact that Easter Sunday was only three days before the time of the accused incident, which was said to have happened on March 19 and Easter Sunday was March 22, 1992. Considering the large number of people who would turn out for shopping in that parking lot, not a single person at any time came forward as a witness. A reasonable person would think at least one man or woman would have shown up as a witness and come forward should such person was observed a full-grown man showing his private body to a young girl. However, not a single person came forward. Based on those grounds, Davis thought that he would be set free. Second, Davis rested his confidence on the fact that he was never arrested, and Thirdly, Davis was denied the right to be represented by an attorney, which caused Davis to serve as his own lawyer—Pro Se.

On December 21, 1993, Davis got his shocking News; the North Carolina Court of Appeals handed its decision affirming his conviction rendered by the Superior court. However, in the alternative, Davis petitioned the Supreme Court of North Carolina for Discretionary Review of the opinion of North

Carolina Court of Appeal. Unfortunately, the State Supreme Court did not consider the case, and therefore, the conviction was never overturned.

At this junction, Davis, as a history and government teacher, had the question in his mind, What explanation could be provided to his students regarding tacking matters to be resolved in the courts rather than taking matters into their own hands?

DAVIS'S ADVERSITY MOVED INTO HIS TEACHER CAREER

Davis's Adversity was extended for deeper than the unlawful ground of bring him to court in violation of his civil rights protected under both State and Federal Constitutions, which is described as Davis's Second Assault which involved removing Davis from his teaching profession.

As with the court system of having brought Davis to trial with not having been arrested, and no warrant.

The Public School Board of Robeson County brought Davis before a School Board for a dismissal hearing where there was no complaint filed against Davis with the School Board. Davis Never had any complaints against him at any time during his teaching career, and Davis was named as Teacher of the Year at his School, which involved the school faculty and students selecting the Teacher of the Year.

Attorney Arnold Locklear was the School Board attorney and served as the School Board attorney in the prosecution at all times during the dismissing hearing of Davis. The School Board dismissal of Davis was completely in violation of North Carolina General Statute, codified at G.S. Sec. 11Sc-325 (f1), and required an investigation. The Robeson School Board members admitted through their attorney Arnold Locklear conducted no investigation as required Under North Carolina Stature, 115c- 325(j) (5), which required the school board to share materials that would be introduced against Davis before and at the school dismissal hearing. Furthermore, the dismissal of Davis's teaching employment was biased, arbitrary, and capricious in violation of protection of North Carolina Tenure Act and due process Provisions and the United States' Constitution and the Constitution of North Carolina. No complaint was ever filed with the Robeson County School Board, and no document of a charge of any matter was served upon Davis. However, School Board Attorney Arnold Locklear admitted in a deposition that there was never any investigation made regarding of any matter relating to Davis.

FEDERAL UNITED STATES DISTRICT COURT TERRANCE BOYLE ENTERED THE GAIN OF FEDERAL CRIMINALS

The Criminal Actions engaged under the federal judgeship of Judge Terrance W. Boyle had been summitted to the United States Justice Department pursuant to Title 18 U.S.C. Section 2382 to report the treasonous acts, neglect of his legal and statutory duty malfeasance, misfeasance, and nonfeasance of the United States District Court. Eastern District Judge Terrance Boyle, who has violated the United States Constitution and its Amendments, and who has conspired with two defendants who were named in Davis's Lawsuit filed in the United States District Court, Eastern District of North Carolina on the date of April 25, 2019. Namely G. Bryan Collins Jr., along with Assistant Court Clerk Tasha O'Neal, currently serving in the Wake County Superior Court Clerk's office to violate the United States Constitution.

IN RELATIONS TO THE TWO ABOVE-NAMED STATE COURT OFFICIALS HAD IN DIRECT RELATION WITH THE TREASONOUS ACTION ENGAGED BY FEDERAL DISTRICT COURT JUDGE TERRANCE W. BOYLE

On January 16, 2016, Davis came on to learn that all of his retirement funds were stolen from the North Carolina Treasury Department/Retirement Systems Division. Davis made every effort possible to acquire information concerning the removal of his retirement funds. Davis filed a request to appear before the Fraud, Abuse and Waste Committee within the North Carolina Treasury Department. Davis's efforts to go before the Fraud, Abuse and Waste Committee were blocked by certain persons within the Treasury Department, assisted by North Carolina Superior Court Judge G. Bryan Collins Jr. and a Deputy Clerk, Tosha O'Neal, with the Superior Court of Wake County, North Carolina.

On April 25, 2019, Davis filed his Civil Complaint against Judge Collins and Deputy Clerk O'Neal in the United States District Court, under Title 42 U.S.C. Section 1983 For the Eastern District Of North Carolina Southern Division Case File Number *Davis v. Collins et al.* 7:19-CV-81-BO (Assigned Judge to that Case—Terrance W. Boyle). The reader of this book is requested to Watch step by step as to how Judge Boyle Criminally Obstructed Justice: On or about April 26, 2019, Judge Boyle in Ex Parte (Outside of Court) removed Davis's Lawsuit from the Court and by Order directed the Court Clerk, Peter Moore, to inform the two named defendants of the above-named case not to answer the Complaint and to disregard the summons which were served upon them. A copy of Judge Terrance Boyle's Order is filed with the Clerk of the United States District Court. Consequently, Judge Terrance Boyle acted as the attorney and judge at the same time for an unlawful purpose to the benefit of those Defendants named in Davis's lawsuit. Take notice, Judge Terrance Boyle adopted a means to hide his criminal action with obstruction of Justice, of which the unlawful judge obtained a check in the amount of four hundred dollars, of which judge noted as a Refund given to Davis. A copy of that check is listed herein—See Document "A." However, Davis refused to cash such check, which he considered to be a fraud to protect criminal action.

Davis's question has at all times bud his mind: What Factors waged upon Judge Terrance Boyle caused him to Obstruct Justice by blocking Davis's Lawsuit when such critical matter of stealing Retirement Funds from the North Carolina Treasure Department/Retirement System Divisions. At some point in time, a thought came into Davis's mind which contained two Factors: First Factor—No one can get money out of the State Treasury Department in absence of the State Treasurer and without the approval of the Board of Trustees, and the Second Factor rested upon the question, Who was the State Treasurer during the stealing of Davis's Retirement Funds From the State Treasury Department/Retirement Systems Division?

During the very period of that question, Davis was coming out of the United States Post Office on Fayetteville Street, Raleigh, NC, and about the time Davis had approached the steps, all of a sudden, the ANSWER: "Harlan Boyles!" which hit Davis like a ball of lightning, to the degree Davis almost fell down the steps of that post office based on the fact that Mr. Harlan Boyle served this state as its Treasurer for more than twenty years with an Exalted Name and was known as the Keeper of the Purse.

Nevertheless, Davis went to his car parked on Blount Street and got in his car with his eyes filled with water, but yet attempting to drive home, located in Lumberton, NC, with the thought that a state patrolman might end up serving him with a traffic ticket because the water in his eyes was obstructing his vision. Nevertheless, Davis made it to Exit 49 off 95 South and spent about forty minutes setting in his car with hopes to have found a Treasurer to whom he could point out as the thief who stole his retirement funds. Then at a certain moment, the thought came, "Owl, Good Buddy, you got it." Davis remarked loud enough as if a person was within five feet from his car with Davis speaking to himself: "Yes! I got it, Harlan Boyles, the Thief." Davis thought he was ready to head home and backed his car less than five inches, of which his mindset changed quickly. "No way!" Even if a thousand Devils out of hell told you that, you should not and will not believe that lie. Even unto this day, Davis believes that is the truth and nothing but the truth. Nevertheless, Mr. Harlan Boyles was the State Treasurer During the time of which Davis's Retirement Funds were removed from the North Carolina treasury/Retirement Systems Division.

Now, the question remains: why did Judge Terrance Boyle unlawfully enter the Clerk's office and remove Davis's lawsuit from out of the court and on April 26, 2019, unlawfully ordered the Court Clerk, Mr. Peter Moore, to advise the defendants not to answer Davis's Lawsuit and to disregard the summons which were served upon them by the Wake County Sheriff's Office. Clearly, by Judge Boyle's Order, the Clerk's office was forced to participate in the action of Obstruction of justice, which is also a crime committed by Judge Terrance W. Boyle.

CRIMES BY NUMBER OF PERJURY COMMITTED BY JUDGE TERRANCE BOYLE WHICH ARE GROUNDS TO BE REMOVE FROM OFFICE

The reader of this book will take notice of the following civil complaints filed in the Federal Court regarding the consistent violation of Davis's constitutional rights protected under both the state and federal Constitutions.

At this juncture, Davis wants to answer a question that might be raised to him, such as, "Davis, why not just leave all of that alone?" Davis's anticipated answer, based on 18 U.S.C. Section 2382, Misprision of Treason, states: Whoever, owing allegiance to the United States and having knowledge of the commission of any treason against them, conceals and does not, as soon as may be, disclose and make known the same to the President or some judge of the United States, or to the governor or some judge or justice of a particular state is guilty of misprision of treason and shall be fined under this title or imprisoned not more than seven years, or both. As a matter of fact, for over one hundred and sixty years, the United States Supreme Court has repeatedly and consistently held that judges who act without jurisdiction are engaged in treason. The United States Supreme Court provided Judge Terrance W. Boyle and all other judges, state and federal, with this commanding directive, "We (Judges) have no more right to decline the exercise of jurisdiction, which is given, than to usurp that which is not given. The one or the other would be treason to the constitution." Cited in *US v. Will*, 449 U.S. 200, 216, 101 S. Ct. 471, 66 L.Ed. 2d 392, 406 (1980); *Cohens v. Virginia*, 19 U.S. (6 Wheat) 264, 404, 5 Led 257 (1821).

ATTACHMENT DOCUMENT "A"

CRIMINAL COMPLAINT FILED AGAINST A FEDERAL DISTRICT COURT JUDGE, HONORABLE TERRENCE W. BOYLE, WHO SITS ON THE EASTERN DISTRICT OF NORTH CAROLINA SOUTHERN DIVISION

Filed by:
ROBERT L. DAVIS,
United States Citizen
40 Kensington Street
Lumberton, NC 28358
Phone: 910-734-7359
Email: rbobdavis2@aol.com
March 30, 2021

Honorable Merrick Garland
ATTORNEY GENERAL
U.S. Department of Justice
950 Pennsylvania Avenue, N W
Washington DC 20530-0001

Charge of Treason and Misprision of Treason
by Federal District Judge Terrance Boyle
Eastern District of North Carolina

Dear Attorney General Garland:

I am presenting this Criminal Complaint to your attention pursuant to Title 18 U.S.C. Section 2382 to report the treasonous acts, neglect of the above-named federal judge's legal and statutory duty of malfeasance, misfeasance, and nonfeasance of Federal District Court Judge Terrence W Boyle, who has violated the US Constitution and its Amendments and who has conspired with a North Carolina State Superior Court Judge. Therefore, the Grounds on Which I, Robert L. Davis (Hereinafter, "Complainant"), Brings This Criminal Complaint Under Penalty Of Contempt Pursuant to United States Title 18 U.S.C. Sec. 1746 Predicated Upon Charges committed by Federal District Court Judge Terrance W. Boyle (Hereinafter, "Subject Judge") neglect of his legal and statutory duty malfeasance, misfeasance, and nonfeasance of the United States Federal Subject Judge who has violated the US Constitution and its Amendments and who conspired with Russell G. Walker, a North Carolina Superior Court Judge, who also violated the US Constitution and its Amendments, Treasonous acts, and Misprision of Treason with "Subject Judge" in Absence of all Jurisdiction, and Such Actions Were committed by Subject Judge Knowingly with Corruption for Purpose to Obstruct Justice and Did Obstruct Justice As Listed **In Grounds A** through **Ground F**, simultaneously violated Complainant's Civil Rights protected under the Constitution of the United States proceeded by Supporting FACTS Stated Briefly without citing case law. However, Complainant will point to United States Title Codes and the US Constitution, which provide authenticity for the purpose to show that this Complaint is brought forth in good faith and with a list of creditable Witnesses, Addresses, and Phone Numbers who can verify to the Facts listed in This Criminal Complaint. Supporting Documents are attached as well.

A. Ground One: The Subject Judge Knowingly engaged Conspiracy with a North Carolina State Superior Court Judge who waged war upon the Constitution of the United States as related to Case File Number *North Carolina v. Robert Lee Davis* 92 CRS 5565 on the date of April 14, 1993.

Supporting Facts 1: BACKGROUND OF THE SUBJECT JUDGE'S UNLAWFUL ACTION

On April 13, 1993, a North Carolina State Superior Court Judge, Russell G. Walker, Presiding Judge on North Carolina Judicial District Nineteen B, unlawfully came to North Carolina Judicial District Sixteen for purpose to illegally force and did force Complainant into an unlawful criminal court procedure without having been designated by North Carolina Administrative Office of the Courts. Therefore, Subject judge violated federal statutory law by providing shelter to the above-named state superior court judge for interfering with the state judicial system in absence of all jurisdictions on the dates of April 13, 14 and 15, 1993. **Supporting Fact**: On the date of April 13, 1993, Complainant received a shocking letter from the Assistant District Attorney ordering Compliant to appear in the Robeson County Superior Court for a criminal trial where was never arrested; no documented papers with affidavit were ever served upon Complainant. However, later that evening on the above said 13th date of April 1993, Complainant filed a handwritten motion in the office of the Clerk for discovery for purpose to see what if anything he was charged with, who would testify again him. On the very next day, April 14, 1993, Complainant was forced to criminal superior court for trial and on the same day, Presiding Unauthorized Judge Russell G. Walker wrote his Order on Complainant's handwritten Motion denying Complainant's Motion for Discovery. A copy of the said handwritten motion with the named illegal judge's Order is attached as Document "A." Just as the jury was preparing to go into deliberation, Judge Russell Walker told the Jury Complainant confessed at the police station and therefrom Complainant voluntary went to the magistrate's office and confessed of having committed a crime of indecent exposure[1]. Complainant has absolutely no idea where that illegal judge got such false information. A copy of the court transcript with the judge's statement to the jury is attached as Document "B".

B. Ground TWO: The Subject Judge was well aware of the crime of Perjury where the named illegal state judge allowed a young girl named Jamie M.

[1] The district attorney nor did any other person provided such incriminated statement as was made by the presiding judge.

Floyd to commit such perjury under oath in the jury box saying she became so sick, claiming that she went to a doctor and further saying she missed a lot of days out of school as a resort of the alleged indecent exposure. Supporting Facts: The Subject Judge named in this Criminal Complaint will admit of his knowledge concerning the perjury based on the fact that he had sworn documents as to the illegal involvement of state Judge Russell G. Walker[2] that were allowed by the teenage girl, Jamie Michell Floyd, where the girl lied, claiming she became very sick as a result of the allegation against Complainant exposing his private body, of which she claimed happened on March 19, 1992, to where the girl claimed she went to a doctor and that she missed many days out of school. The fact is, the girl did not visit a doctor at all. As aforementioned, Complainant was denied discovery. However, following the trial, Complainant visited the Lumberton High School Principal and obtained a copy of the young girl, Jamie Floyd's, attendance record, which reveals the true fact that the young girl, Jamie Floyd, did not miss a single day out of school from the 17th day of March through the remaining of the '91-92 school year. A copy of the aforementioned girl's attendance record is attached as Document "C."

C. Ground Three: The Subject Judge engaged Obstruction of Justice by providing shelter and hiding the criminal actions of the above-mentioned illegally named state superior court judge for allowing a Lumberton, NC, police officer Don Ward to commit perjury under oath in the jury box at the said unlawful criminal trial.

Supporting Facts: At the April 14, 1993, Criminal trial, a Lumberton Police Officer, Don Ward, was present in the Superior Court Room; for reason,

---

[2] During the latter days of June 1996, North Carolina Superior court Judge Russell G. Walker was in court section in Rowan County Superior Court in what was said to have been a Murder trial of which during that conversation the spoke with what appeared to have a very sad period for that judge for the way he had handled Complainant's trial. Judge Walker provided Complainant with the knowledge of how to filed a Motion for Appropriate Relief under North Carolina General Statute ISA-1415 and 1420, of which Complainant filed the same in the Robeson County Clerk's Office on July 15, 1996. For that, Complainant appreciated that judge.

Complainant was never informed of such police officer would be present at the aforementioned Criminal Trial, was asked to come forward and placed on the jury stand and produced lies under oath saying that he (Ward) served an arrest warrant upon Complainant. Upon cross-examination where Complainant asked Officer Ward the following questions 1: "Did you issue an arrest warrant?" Ward's answer: "When I got to the Magistrate's Office that night there was one issued"; question 2: "Who did you issue an arrest warrant upon?" Ward's answer: "The warrant was taken on Robert Davis"; question 3: "Who did you issued to Mr. Ward?" Ward's answer: "I didn't issue a Warrant to anybody. The warrant was issued to me by the Magistrate on Robert Davis, and it was served on Robert Davis." A portion copy of the transcript record is attached as Document "D." Fact, no one issued a warrant on Robert Davis, this Complainant.

<u>Further Supporting Facts:</u> On April 25, 1994, Robeson County Superior Court Judge Joe Freeman Britt acted outside of a court hearing in ex parte, arrested Complainant. By information provided by the Prosecuting Assistant District Attorney, told Complainant in the parking lot of the US. Post Office saying (Judge) Joe Britt met with Frankie G. Floyd, Mother of the young Jamie Floyd, and requested Joe Britt to place Complainant in prison. Complainant remained in prison for about fifteen days. Further, Complainant was placed on probation for one year and paid a fine of five hundred dollars to the Clerk's Office. As of this day, Complainant does not know why he was placed in prison by said Judge Britt as to a legal ground. The Subject Judge has not made a single word concerning Complainant's false imprisonment and this issue has never been analyzed.

<u>D. Ground Four</u>: Subject Judge's filed a fraudulent Memorandum for purpose to harm Complainant's character.

<u>Supporting Facts</u>: On August 27, 1998, Subject Judge sent out a Memorandum to the United States Marshal's Service, the FBI, and every judge in the Eastern District of North Carolina, Southern Division, saying "this letter is considered a threat." However, Subject Judge never identified the "This Letter." A copy of the Subject Judge's Memorandum is attached as Document "E."

That on September 3, 1998, United States Deputy Marshal, Kelvin Stone, came to Complainant's home without a warrant nor any document. Deputy Stone informed Complainant of an order by Subject Judge directed Stone to Complainant's home to warn Complainant of an arrest was to be made against Complainant if Complainant filed another lawsuit in the federal court. Pursuant to Federal Titles 18 U.S.C. Sections 241 and 2382, the Subject judge committed felonious crime as an attack upon the Constitution of the United States.

Further Intimidation by Subject Judge: On September 7, 2018, two US Marshal Deputies arrived at Complainant's home with a message saying Subject Judge directed them to warn Complainant that he would be placed under arrest if Complainant filed a lawsuit in the United States District Court Eastern District of North Carolina. One of the two Marshal Deputes identified his last name as Brewington. On the same above date, Complainant reported the crime to the Lumberton Police Department. A copy of the Police Report is Attached as Document "F."

E. Ground Four: Complainant became a victim as a result all of his state retirement funds were stolen from the North Carolina State Treasury/Retirement Systems Division Account. Subject Judge's Father was the state Treasurer during this period of time.

Supporting Facts: On January 16, 2016, Complainant came on to learn that all of his retirement funds having been stolen from the North Carolina Treasury Department/Retirement Systems Division. Complainant made every effort possible to acquire information concerning the removal of his retirement fund. Complainant filed a request to appear before the Fraud, Abuse and Waste Committee within the North Carolina Treasury Department. Complainant's effort to go before the Fraud, Abuse and Waste Committee were blocked by certain persons within the Treasury Department assisted by North Carolina Superior Court Judge G. Bryan Collins Jr. and a Deputy Clerk, Tosha O'Neal, with the Superior Court of Wake County, NC. On April 25, 2019, Complainant filed his civil Complaint against Judge Collins and Deputy Clerk O'Neal in the above said Federal District Court, Case file Number *Davis v. Collins et al.* 7: 19-CV- 81-BO. As to this named civil action, Subject Judge Knowingly Obstructed Justice.

Supporting Facts: On or about April 26, 2019, Subject Judge in Ex Parte removed Complainant's Lawsuit from the Court and by Order directed the Court Clerk, Peter Moore, to inform the two defendants of the above-named case not to answer the Complaint and to disregard the summons which were served upon them. A Copy of the Subject Judge's Order is on file with the Clerk of the United States District Court. Consequently, Subject Judge acted as the attorney and Judge to the benefit of those Defendants named in the abovenamed Civil Action. As a means to hide the Subject Judge's illegal action, Subject Judge obtained a Check in the amount of four hundred dollars, noted as a Refund given to this Complainant. A copy of the said is attached as Document "G".

On August 21, 2019, Complainant Filed his Civil Action File Number *Davis v. Judge Terrence W. Boyle* 7: 19-MC-6-D against Subject Judge for the violation of his civil rights protected under the United States Constitution. However, this Named Civil Action was blocked by Federal District Judge, Honorable James Dever, who is a presiding judge with the United States District Court for the Eastern District of North Carolina Southern Division.

By date December 19, 2019, the Deputy Clerk issued an Order holding that the clerk not to accept any further filings from Complainant. Copy of the Deputy Clerk's Order is attached as Document "H."

F. Ground Five: Through out every Ground of Obstruction of Justice, Subject Judge Lied under his oath as a reason for blocking Complainant's lawsuits by sheltering, hiding, and/or assisting law violators by engaging PERJURY.

Supporting Facts: Subject Judge lied relating to his Orders holding, saying Complainant previous issues filed with federal courts had been analyzed. The Subject Judge referees to the following ISSUES: 1. Brought to Criminal court without a warrant, denied an attorney, denied discovery, falsely imprisoned, perjury admitted at trial, illegal judge came to judicial district without designation, loss of Complainant's career teacher occupation.[3] The Subject Judge cannot point to a single order where a single issue had been Analyzed. In fact, NOT ONE OF THOSE ISSUES APPEAR WITHIN A Court's Orders that THE Subject Judge LISTED. The Subject Judge also presented his same Lies to the Chief Judge of the Fourth Circuit Court.

The Subject Judge Is Not Above the LAW. (Emphasis Added) Finally, the following damage was done to Complainant: 1. Complainant was illegally convicted; 2, Was Falsely imprisoned; 3, Illegally removed from his career teacher employment and lost his pastorate from his assigned church. Therefore, Complainant became unemployed. However, on December 3, 1992, the Robeson County School Board directed the School Superintendent to expunge Complainant's records. Unfraternally, Complainant has never been brought back into his teaching career other than an apology by the Tommy D. Sweat, then-Chairman of the School Board for the Public Schools of Robeson County at the time of Complainant's dismissal from his teaching employment—about ten years later the apology made. However, the School Board Superintendent verbally apologized to Complainant regarding his dismissal. A copy of the said school board letter is attached as Document "I." The Subject Judge of this Complaint has always known these facts since 1998 because the Subject Judge was assigned to the Civil Case File No. *Davis v. The Public Schools of Robeson County* 7:98-CV-128-BO (1). A Copy of the Subject Judge's Order is Attached as Document "J."

Finally in 1998, Complainant filed a civil complaint regarding his illegal trial without an arrest warrant, denied the right to be represented by an attorney and his illegal dismissal from his teaching career. However, on the 7th day of September 2018, Complainant's lawsuit File No. *Robert L Davis, Plaintiff v. Russell Walker, et al.*, 7:98-CV-116-D was reassigned by Court Order. A Copy of the Reassignment Order is attached as Document "K." No action has been taken on the Court Reassignment Order. However, by letter, Complainant received a

[3] The Public Schools of Robeson County directed the Superintendent to expunge Complainant.

letter from Mr. Joshua B. Royster, Assistant United States Attorney, identifying that he is the Attorney for the Subject Judge Reassigned Civil Action. A Copy of the said Attorney is attached in respect of the attorney.

Based on the Subject Judge's and the deputy Clerk's Order, Complainant is denied his US Constitutional Rights to file a motion requesting action upon the reassigned Case. A Copy of the Deputy Clerk is attached as Document "L."

Summitted By:
Robert L. Davis
March 31, 2021

"A"
In the Superior Court

92 CRS 5565
Robert L. Davis
v.
State of North Carolina
Robert L. Davis, defendant, moves the court pursuant to criminal case file 92 C.RS 5565 in preparation for trial set tomorrow at 9:30 a.m. in superior court by Jury, on this motion further moves the court for discovery in this matter.
This the 13th day of April 1993.
Robert L. Davis

Robert L. Davis
Pro Se
40 (?) street
(?), N.C. 28358
4/14/93 Motion is without merit. Case not within original Jurisdiction of Superior Court (15A-901) Therefore no right to discovery.
RGW Aucer
Judge Presiding

"B"
St. vs. Robert L. Davis

THE COURT: Ladies and gentlemen, the Court has ruled the instance of this case, under all the evidence, Mr. Davis voluntarily went with the officers to the police department and there from went voluntarily to the Magistrate's office to-to appear before the Magistrate; under those circumstances no arrest was made and no arrest warrant as required under the law of the State of North Carolina.

"C"
Jamie Floyd sat right here in the courthouse and spoke in terms of the number of times she had to go to the hospital, the doctor's office and psychiatrist because plaintiff exposed himself, but yet instead she would never bring forth any kind of evidence that was ever done, never even went to the doctor's office. And the

plaintiff even asked for that and it was denied by the Court. And my efforts to gain discovery was by law—- as a matter of fact. North Carolina General Statute 1A1, Rule 26 North Carolina Rules of Civil Procedures gives the plaintiff the right of discovery as well as Rule 45. That is subpoenas were sent out under Rule 45.

What happened then when you sent out rules by rule—sent out that material requested by a plaintiff by affidavit—excuse me, Your Honor, by subpoena? What reason for plaintiff not to gain discovery other than the court said no, we're not going to allow you to have that discovery and it was done by law? I know it's easy to come in and say you didn't file it right and you didn't—for these people to say you didn't file it properly. He is representing his client, and I know according to North Carolina General Statutes 15A 12 32 it just simply says that the judge is to have a—to be in an act of cold neutrality, that is to be in an act of cold

"D"

THE COURT: YOU MAY CROSS-EXAMINE, MR. DAVIS

CROSS-EXAMINATION BY MR. DAVIS

Q. MR. WARD, DID YOU OBTAIN A-AN-AN ARREST WARRANT THAT NIGHT?

A. YES, SIR, I DID.

Q. DID YOU ISSUE AN ARREST WARRANT?

A. WHEN I GOT TO THE MAGISTRATE'S OFFICE THAT NIGHT, THERE WAS ONE ISSUED.

Q. WHO DID YOU ISSUE AN ARREST WARRANT TO?

A. THE WARRANT WAS TAKEN OUT ON ROBERT DAVIS.

Q. WHO DID YOU ISSUE THE WARRANT TO, MR. WARD?

A. I DIDN'T ISSUE A WARRANT TO ANYBODY. THE WARRANT WAS ISSUED TO ME BY THE MAGISTRATE ON ROBERT DAVIS, AND IT WAS SERVED ON ROBERT DAVIS.

Q. WHEN DID YOU SERVE A WARRANT?

A. AFTER IT WAS OBTAINED.

Q. DO YOU HAVE A COPY OF THE WARRANT THAT WAS OBTAINED AND ISSUED?

A. NO, SIR, I DON'T.

Q. WHY DON'T YOU HAVE ONE, MR. WARD?

A. IT'S NOT STANDARD PROCEDURE FOR US TO KEEP A COPY OF THE WARRANT.

Q. THE FACT OF IT IS YOU NEVER ISSUED A WARRANT, ISN'T THAT RIGHT?

Robert L. Davis
40 Kensington Street
Lumberton, NC 28358
March 31, 2021

Joe Biden, President
United States of America
1600 Pennsylvania Avenue, NW
Washington, DC 20500

Dear President Biden:

Please note that I am sending a copy of the Criminal Complaint of which has been sent to US Attorney Genera I Merrick Garland, of which consists of serious felonious crimes against the United States Constitution of America.

Mr. President, please read this Criminal Complaint with your mind Focused primarily on the treasonous acts waged against Our Nation. In other Words, this Complaint is not about Robert Davis, this person. However, I have a Civil Lawsuit pending with the United States District Court, Eastern District of North Carolina, Eastern Division.

With Great Concern,
-Robert L. Davis,
US Citizen

(order?)

Stroud, Angel E. Gray, Michele Sykes, and Barbara Baldwin were actors in a joint conspiracy and developed fraudulent documents with Davis's name fraudulently attached to those documents and defendants which falsely accused Davis of having taken his funds from out of his retirement account. Those fraudulent documents were produced for purpose to hide the truth from Davis regarding his stolen property. This state case gave birth to the federal lawsuit, which the state superior Court judge protected those defendants from answer to Davis's Complaint. As a result, Davis took his case to the US District Court Eastern District of North Carolina, which caused this matter to be assigned to Judge Boyle.

Therefore, Judge Boyle waged war upon the United States Constitution, and Judge Boyle did so without jurisdiction. Title 28 U.S.C. Section 295 says: "parties shall have jurisdiction," citing *Old Wayne Mut. Life Assoc. v. Mcdonough*, 204 U.S. 8, 27 S. Ct. 236 (1907); *Scott v. Mcneal*, 154 U.S. 34,14 S. Ct. 1108 (1894); *Pennoyer v. Neff.* 95 U.S. 714, 733 (1877).

Due Process is a requirement of the US Constitution. Violation of the United States Constitution by a judge deprives that person from being a judge under the law. He/She is acting as a private person and not in the capacity of being a judge. Judge Terrance Boyle's took action by removing Davis's Complaint from the Clerk's office and by Order blocking Davis from ever bring able to file any lawsuit he may want to file in the United States District Court. Therefore, Judge Terrance Boyle was not a judge but a private citizen according United State Supreme Court ruling.

The United States Supreme Court ruled saying, "Engaging in an act of treason against the United States Constitution by any citizen of the United States is an act of war against the United States, *Cooper v. Aaron*, 358 U.S. 1, 78 S.Ct.1401(1958). All enlisted personnel of the US Military, the National Guard, all US attorneys, all members of US Senate and US House of Representatives, and all Cabinet secretaries have taken the following oath of office:

"I ___ do solemnly swear (or affirm) that I will support and defend the Constitution of the United States against all enemies, foreign or domestic; that I will bear true faith and allegiance to the same..."

Finally, Davis asked that his rights as a citizen be restored to enter the federal district Court for redress and allow any issues filed with the courts be determined based on the merits. Most important, give order to protect the integrity of our Nation Judicial System.

Yours truly,
Robert L. Davis
RLD/sm

cc: Senate Judicial Committee
House Judicial Committee
US Attorney General
Special in Charge
US Senators
Chief Justice
Eastern District Clerk
Judicial Committee
Lindsey Graham
Jerrold Nadler
William Barr
FBI Richmond, VA
Richard Burr/Tom Tillis
Honorable John Roberts
Peter Moore
4th Circuit Court, Richmond, VA

Robert L. Davis, Citizen of the United States
40 Kensington Street
Lumberton, NC 28358
910-734-7359
Email: rbobdavis2@aol.com
September 5, 2018

Honorable Judge Terrance W. Boyle
Associate Judge
United States District Court
Eastern District of North Carolina
320 New Bern Avenue Ste 174
Raleigh, NC 27601
Re: **REQUEST FOR ANSWERS**

Dear Honorable Judge Boyle,

Let me begin by informing you of my fortune for having talked with Mr. Peter A. More, District Court Clerk, Yesterday. Mr. More stated to me in our conversation that I should write a letter to you, and Mr. More continued to say that you would not mind if I wrote a letter addressed to you.

Now, Judge, why was that such a big deal? Answer: The way you handled my lawsuits that were before your court, I saw you as a racist, especially against This Black Man, and considering that some years ago you state that Jessy Helms was your image to whom you looked up to and that same person recommended you to President George H. Bush to be a Nominee to the United States Supreme Court, and God Bless America, That Never Happened.

That having been said, please provide an answer to each of the following questions regarding Civil Action filed against North Carolina State Superior Court Judge Russell G. Walker 7:98-CV-128-B0(1):

NORTH CAROLINA
7915 Microsoft Way
CHARLOTTE, NC 28273

David Scott
Section Chief
Public Correction and Civil Rights Section

A LIST OF WITNESSES DAVIS PROVIDED WITH THE FBI, WHO COULD VERY WELL BE HELPFUL TO THE FBI INVESTIGATION REGARDING TO THE PRECISE FACTS PROVIDED IN THE CRIMINAL REPORT ATTACHED AS DOCUMENT "A"

1. Kelvin Stone, a United States Deputy. Stone can or will witness to the fact that United States District Court Judge Terrance W. Boyle sent him to Davis's home on the date of September 3, 1998, to inform Davis of an arrest would be made Davis if he filed another lawsuit in the federal court. Kelvin Stone may be contacted by way of the US Marshal.

2. North Carolina state Superior Court Judge G. Bryan Collins, who can or will witness to the fact that Judge Terrance Boyle protected him by way of court order from answering Davis's Lawsuit by taking the criminal action of entering the Clerk's office in ex parte and leaned to his favor to protect and did protect him from providing answer to Robert Davis's Lawsuit, of which Judge Boyle removed the same from the Clerk's Office and that Judge Boyle allowed him to disregard the summons that were served on him.

3. The Top officer with the United States Marshal can or will testify to the fact that Judge Terrance Boyle, on two occasions, sent Marshall Deputies to Davis's home with threats of placing Davis in Prison if he filed a lawsuit in the Federal Courts. Those threats were made at Davis's own home on the dates of September 3, 1998, and on September 7, 2018. Judge Terrance Boyle sent two Marshals to Davis's home with threats of placing Davis in prison if Davis

filed another lawsuit with the federal court. One of those Marshal Deputies identified his last name as "Brewington."

3. Shannon Wharry, manage with the Fraud, Abuse Waste Committee, will testify to the fact that Davis filed his complaint to be heard with respect to his stolen retirement funds and that the Plaintiff was denied by Thomas Causey's letter, aided by other party members named in case No. 18 CVS 15535.

4. Jeff Cardin, with the Retirement Systems Personnel Manager of the Call Center, will testify to the fact that Judge Terrance Boyle's Father was North Carolina State Treasurer during the time Davis's Retirement Funds were stolen from the North Carolina Retirement Systems. However, Mr. Cardin will state to the fact that he has no information as to how the funds went missing.

5. United States District Court Clerk Peter Moore will or can testify to the fact that United States Federal Judge Terrance Boyle ordered him to commit a felonious crime to remove Davis's Lawsuit out of the Clerk's office and inform the defendants in civil action 19 cv 006586 to disregard the summons that were served upon them.

ROBERT L. DAVIS
PLAINTIFF Pro Se.

ROBERT L DAVIS
40 Kensington Street
Lumberton, NC 28358
Rbobdavis2@aol.com
910-734-7359

February 17, 2022

Criminal Complaint To: Honorable Chief Judge Richard E. Myers
United States District Court
For the Eastern District of North Carolina
Southern Division
ADDRESS: 1003 South 17th Street
Wilmington, North Carolina 28401
Copies Of This Criminal Complaint Are Provided
To The Following Persons: David Scott, U.S.
Department of Justice
Directed to Criminal Division

Samuel W. Phillips
Circuit Executive
United States Court of Appeals
Fourth Circuit
1100 East Main Suite 617
Richmond, Virginia 2319-3517

CRIMINAL COMPLAINT

Dear Honorable Chief Judge Myers:

This Criminal Charge of Treason and Misprision of Treason by Two Federal Judges whose names are Terrance W. Boyle and James C. Dever 111 both of whom serve on the United States District Court for the Eastern District Of North Carolina, Southern Division.

INTRODUCTION

THE TWO NAMED FEDERAL JUDGES, TERRENCE W. BOYLE AND JAMES C. DEVEL 111 ARE ALLEGED OF HAVING COMMITTED A NUMBER OF CRIMES AGAINST THE CONSTITUTION OF THE UNITED STATES. BASED ON LAW WHICH THE FEDERAL STATUTES AND THE UNITED STATES SUPREME COURT AUTHENTICALLY HOLD SUCH ACTS COMMITTED BY THESE ABOVE NAMED TWO FEDERAL JUDGES AS TREASONOUS ACTS AGAINST THE UNITED STATES CONSTITUTION.

I, Robert L. Davis, a citizen of the United States and a Resident of Lumberton, N. Carolina bring forth this Criminal Complaint to your attention and to those Honorable persons whose names are listed herein above. Robert L. Davis (Hereinafter and at all times referred to as "Complainant") in regards to this Criminal Complaint. Therefore, Complainant believes that it is his responsibility to bring this Criminal Complaint Pursuant to United States Titles 18 Sections 241 and 2382 to report Federal Crimes of which federal statutes and the United States Supreme Court declare to be Treasonous acts, neglect of those two named Judges legal and statutory duties malfeasance, misfeasance, nonfeasance of both federal judges named herein have violated the United States Constitution and its Amendments and by the same.

FIRST CRIMINAL ACTION: On the dates of April 13, 14 and 15, 1993, the stage was set which created a path way in which Federal District Court Judge Terrence Boyle came on to engage very serious treasonous acts against the United States Constitution in a conspiracy with a North Carolina State Superior Court Judge who also engaged treasonous actions against both the Constitution of North Carolina and the Constitution of the United States.

FACTS: On April 13, 1993, North Carolina State Superior Court Judge Russell G. Walker who lived and presided on North Carolina 19th Judicial District unlawfully assigned himself to North Carolina Judicial District 16th Judicial District without designation as required by law and in absence of jurisdiction forced Complainant into a Robeson County Superior Court, Lumberton, North Carolina to be tried and was tried on what unlawful Private Citizen Walker told the jury saying Complainant was on trial for an act of indecent exposure. However, Private Citizen Walker knew that Complainant was never served with a warrant of such crime, and no criminal complaint was ever filed with a law enforcement officer against complainant relating to any crime and Private Citizen Walker knew or should have known that he had lost his jurisdiction as a judge. And, Complainant never committed such crime nor any other crime. However, Private Citizen Walker in **ABSENCE OF ALL JURISDICTION** forced Complainant into the unlawful court less than 24 hours prior to the court trial. Where, upon the said 13th day of April, 1993, Complainant quickly wrote a hand written Motion and filed the same with the Superior Court Clerk's Office for Discovery for purpose to see what he was accused of and who would testify against him. Private Citizen Russell Walker wrote an Order on Complainant's hand written Motion which unlawfully prevented Complainant's Motion for Discovery. A copy of Complainant's hand written Motion with Private Citizen Walker's Order of denial written on the same is attached as Exhibit "A". Secondly, just before the jury went to the jury room for deliberation, Private Citizen Walker testified to the Jury saying: **Complainant went to the police department voluntary and therefrom to the Magistrate's Office and confessed and Walker told the Jury saying that under the circumstance North Carolina did not require an arrest warrant to be issued;** that statement was an act of a **crime of Perjury** and the same was supported by federal Judge Terrence W. Boyle which resulted to as **treason against the United States Constitution.** A copy of the Court Transcript with Private Citizen Walker's incriminating statement made to the jury is hereby attached herein as Exhibit "B" and adopted the same as if written in this Criminal Complaint.

Walker allowed a 15-year-old girl, Named Jamie Michell Floyd to take the witness stand and lied on the jury stand saying Complainant exposed his private part toward her in a large Parking lot, so **named as Biggs Parking lot**. However, never named a particular place in the said parking lot where said claimed crime to have happened nor could a single witness be found and brought especially considering two factors: Biggs Parking shopping Center during the time of 1992 was the largest supporting center in Robeson County and secondly, Easter Season was on going and the accused crime of indecent exposure was claimed to have happened on March 19th,1992 openly in that said parking lot. Yet, Judge Boyle knew that not one person could be brought forth as a witness of the accused crime. And, Judge Boyle knew during that unlawful trial where Private Citizen Walker had no Jurisdiction. Therefore, Complainant became a "Victim" resorting from the jury's "verdict of guilty". Complainant was given two years of probation, Sentenced with a jail term for several weeks. Complainant lost his career teaching profession and Complainant was forced by Walker's unlawful court to pay a fine in the amount of $500.00[1]. However, Complainant is filing this complaint for criminal purpose; **NOT A CIVIL COMPLAINT.**

And, here where Judge Terrence W. Boyle engaged his **First Treasonous action** against the United States Constitution where there is no genuine dispute regarding the treasonous actions against the United States Constitution Committed by Judge Terrence W. Boyle as listed herein: 1) Acting as a lawyer and Judge as a protector on behalf of Private Citizen Russell Walker where Judge Terrence W. Boyle had complete knowledge of the fact that Walker unlawfully moved from his assigned jurisdiction 19 and entered Jurisdiction 16. Judge Boyle new to the fact that Walker forced Complainant into a criminal court where Complainant was never charged with a crime and Complainant was never served with a warrant[2]. 2) Judge Boyle was provided with authentic documents with facts that Complainant was denied by Private Citizen Walker to allow him to contact his attorney. Furthermore, Judge Terrence Boyle knew or should have known to the fact that United States Supreme Court ruled holding when a judge acted as a state Citizen; as Walker did without jurisdiction was an act of treason;

---

[1] During the latter days of June 1996, North Carolina Superior Court Judge Russell G. Walker was in a court section in Rowan County in what was said to have been a Murder trial, by a telephone conversation among Judge Walker and Complainant, the said judge spoke with what appeared to have been a very sad period for that judge as for the way he had handled Complainant's trial. Judge Walker provided Complainant with the knowledge of how to file a motion for Appropriate Relief under North Carolina General Statute 15A-1415 and 1420 of which Complainant filed the same in the Robeson County Clerk's Office on July 15, 1996. For that legal assistance, Complainant appreciated judge Walker even to the point that Complainant would have never filed a single complaint against that judge. However, several weeks later, Complainant was in the proximity of Campbell University Law School in which Complainant mentioned this matter to a lawyer who told Complainant about said U.S. Statute 18 Section 2382 which Complainant began to file complaints against said judge.

[2] However, a civil suit was filed against. State Judge Walker in Judge Boyle's court, no issue was addressed. Which in itself appears to be a crime against Judge Boyle who himself should have filed a criminal complaint against state judge Boyle; if in fact Judge Boyle filed no Complaint.

U.S. vs. Will, 449 U.S. 200, 216, 101 S. Ct. 471, 66 L.Ed 2d 392, 406 (1980); **Chens v. Virginia**, 19 U.S. (Wheat) 264, 404, L.Ed 257 (1821).3) Judge Terrence Boyle was provided with full knowledge that Private Citizen Walker chose a young 15 year old girl named Jamie Floyd, to commit perjury under oath in the jury box saying that she became so sick claiming that she went to a doctor and further saying she missed a lot of days out of school as a resort of the alleged indecent exposure.

SUPPORTING FACTS: Judge Boyle will admit of his knowledge concerning the perjury based on the fact that he had sworn documents as to the involvement of Private Citizen Russell G. Walker who allowed the above named teenage girl to lie claiming that she became very sick as a resort of the allegation against Complainant of exposing his private body saying under perjury that she went to a doctor and that she missed many days out of school, and saying that she went to the hospital and went to a psychiatrist and further said that she missed many days out of school. Consequently, the named young girl's father, Philip Floyd went on to the **witness stand and lied under oath in support of his daughter. However, Investigation revealed the fact that the girl did not visit a single doctor at all nor a psychiatrist of whom the girl claimed under a lie saying she went to a psychiatrist as the girl testified with a lie saying Complainant** exposed himself to her. However, by investigation a copy of the young girl, Jamie Floyd's school attendance record was brought forth which revealed the fact that the said young girl did not miss a single day out of school from the 17th day of March throughout the remaining of the '91-92 school year; keeping in mind the indecent exposure was claimed to have occurred on March 19th 1992. A copy of the afore mention girl's attendance record is attached as Document "C". As afore mentioned, Complainant was denied discovery and therefore, Complainant had no way of knowing that such criminal testimony would be brought against him at that illegal trial at the expense of those criminal actors the United States Government. **Therefore, JUDGE BOYLE's engaged crime of obstruction of justice by providing shelter and hiding the criminal actions of the above-mentioned illegal named Russell G. Walker for allowing a Lumberton**, North Carolina Police officer whose name is Don Ward who happened to have been in that court room without a summons of whom Complainant was never informed about an officer named Don Ward was to come to the jury trial and be placed in the witness stand at the said **saying: Complainant went to the police department voluntary and therefrom to the Magistrate's Office and confessed and Walker told the Jury saying that under the circumstance North Carolina did not require an arrest warrant to be issued** that statement was an act of a **crime of perjury** and the same was supported by federal Judge Terrence W. Boyle which resulted to as **treason against the United States Constitution.** A copy of the Court Transcript with Private Citizen Walker's incriminating statement made to the jury is hereby attached herein as Exhibit "B" and adopted the same as if written in this Criminal Complaint.

Judge Terrence Boyle was provided with full knowledge that Private Citizen Walker chose a young 15 year old girl named Jamie Floyd, to commit perjury under oath in the jury box saying that she became so sick claiming that she went to a doctor and further saying she missed a lot of days out of school as a resort of the alleged indecent exposure.

<u>SUPPORTING FACTS:</u> Judge Boyle will admit of his knowledge concerning the perjury based on the fact that he had sworn documents as to the involvement of Private Citizen Russell G. Walker who allowed the above named teenage girl to lie claiming that she became very sick as a resort of the allegation against Complainant of exposing his private body saying under perjury that she went to a doctor and that she missed many days out of school, and saying that she went to the hospital and went to a psychiatrist and further said that she missed many days out of school. Consequently, the named young girl's father, Philip Floyd went on to the **witness stand and lied under oath in support of his daughter. However, Investigation revealed the fact that the girl did not visit a single doctor at all nor a psychiatrist of whom the girl claimed under a lie saying she went to a psychiatrist as the girl testified with a lie saying Complainant** exposed himself to her. However, by investigation a copy of the young girl, Jamie Floyd's school attendance record was brought forth which revealed the fact that the said young girl did not miss a single day out of school from the 17th day of March throughout the remaining of the '91-92 school year; keeping in mind the indecent exposure was claimed to have occurred on March 19th 1992. A copy of the afore mention girl's attendance record is attached as Document "C". As afore mentioned, Complainant was denied discovery and therefore, Complainant had no way of knowing that such criminal testimony would be brought against him at that illegal trial at the expense of those criminal actors of the United States Government. **<u>Therefore, JUDGE BOYLE's engaged crime of obstruction of justice by providing shelter and hiding the criminal actions of the above-mentioned illegal named Russell G. Walker for allowing a Lumberton</u>**, North Carolina Police officer whose name is Don Ward who happened to have been in that court room without a summons of whom Complainant was never informed about an officer named Don Ward was to come to the jury trial and be placed in the witness stand at the said Complainant's unlawful criminal trial to commit perjury and did commit perjury under oath saying that he served an arrest warrant upon Complainant. At this junction, Complainant attaches Police Officer Don Ward's testimony given at that unlawful trial while that Officer was under cross examination as Exhibit "D" and incorporate the same herein by reference.

---

2 However, a civil suit was filed against. State Judge Walker in Judge Boyle's court, no issue was addressed. Which in itself appears to be a crime against Judge Boyle who himself should have filed a criminal complaint against state judge Boyle; if in fact Judge Boyle filed no Complaint.

The Second crime committed by Judge Boyle came by way of the fact that Judge Boyle very well knew of the perjury of which Private Citizen Walker allowed the said name police officer to commit. Moreover, Judge Boyle Committed his **Third Crime while presiding in the Matter of Complainant's Lawsuit regarding Complainant's unlawful dismissal of his teaching career where Judge Boyle upheld Complainant's illegal dismissal of his career profession with the unlawful ruling that protect the named unlawful state judge with an unlawful justification by saying In his Order in case file No. Robert L. Davis v. The Public Schools or Robeson County, et al., No.7:98-CV-128-BO(1) Judge Boyle, saying Complainant "was suspended, and subsequently dismissed, from his teaching position following his arrest on a misdemeanor charge of indecent exposure"**. That very statement was criminal and committed to protect State Private Citizen Russell Walker; subsequently, Judge Boyle was acting as an attorney and a judge at the same time. Judge Boyle Treasonous action is attached as Exhibit "E". That statement was not made by a school board attorney; however, Judge Boyle served as attorney for the Public Schools of Robeson County.[3] A copy of Judge Boyles' statement is hereby attached herein as Document "E" and in cooperated herein by reference.

However, to the contrary, the Robeson County Board Attorney Arnold [illegible]ear confessed in his deposition that no one filed a complaint of any type against Complainant and that more than 90 days had elapsed prior to Complainant's dismissal hearing was set and the state statute required that a teacher's dismissal hearing was required to start prior to the passing of the 90th day. Therefore, Judge Boyle and Judge Devel were so much interested in acting as judge and the attorney for the defense of Robeson County Board of Education and to protect the treasonous act of Judge Russel G. Walker. No lawyer made any attempt to justify the dismissal of Complainant other than acting Judge/ Attorney Terrence W. Boyle.

Again, turning to another phrase of treasonous action by Judge Terrence W. Boyle: The federal crimes reported in this report are brief and specific. On the date of September 7, 2019, the federal judge complained about sent two United States Marshall Agents to the private home of Complainant with intimidation advising The Complainant saying Judge Boyle directed them to advise The Complainant of his arrest and placed behind bars if he filed action in the United States District Court for the Eastern District of North Carolina Southern Division for any reason. Such criminal action falls under United States Code Titles 2382, 241 and 242. On the above stated date, The Complainant reported the criminal act to the Lumberton City Police Department. A copy of the police Report is attached as Document "F"; Next CRIMINAL ACT: On April 25, 2019, The Complainant filed his Civil Complaint with the United States District Court Eastern District of North Carolina Southern Division-Case File No. **Davis v. Collins, et. al., No. 7:19-CV-81-BO. On May 6, 2019,**

Judge Terrence W. Boyle prevented The Complainant's Complaint from going forward in the Federal Court by personally, (In Exparte) removing the Complaint from the Clerk's Office himself and by **Order to the Clerk, Pater Moore, to advise the Parties to the above-named lawsuit not to response to the summons that were served upon them.** And, by Court Order directed the C. rt Clerk to never allow The Complainant to file any documents in the federal court again. Notice the lie judge Boyle employed for his removal of Complainant's lawsuit in Exparta which says, "Robert L Davis is permanently enjoined from filing any new lawsuit, action, proceeding of matter in this Federal District without first obtaining leave of this Court to proceed". A copy of Judge Boyle's Order is attached as Document "G". The case in which Judge Boyle referred is noted as "JUDGEMENT IN A CIVIL CASE" No. 7:97-CV-161-BO, ruled by then Deputy Clerk Lda Gadwim and during the time in which David W. Daniel was the Court Clerk for the United States District Court For the Eastern District of North Carolina, said, "JUDGEMENT" is attached as Exhibit "H". Judge Boyle knew very well that Complainant filed his motion under Penalty of Contempt and the Motion is listed in the Court Records. Therefore, Judge Boyle committed an act of **Perjury**, and such actions fall directly under federal criminal statute Title 18 U.S.C. Section 2382. by the mere fact the judge recruited the federal court clerk to assist him in violating the law and with assault against the Constitution of the United States which resort to Treason and MISPRISION OF TREASON. Complainant Filed notice of Boyle with Judge James Dever. Next CRIMINAL ACT: Judge Boyle Criminally used his office of his judgeship to solicit the Federal District Court Clerk to please the judge by violating The Complainant's federal and state constitutional guaranteed rights. Next CRIMINAL ACT: Perjury committed by Judge Terrence Boyle where the Judge declared that his action to Obstruct the Complainant's lawsuit saying he, Boyle, had entertained the issues set out in The Complainant's lawsuits: **Davis v. The Public Schools of Robeson County of Board of Educ.**, No. 7:98- CV-128-BO(1), the issue in this case involved The Complainant's illegal discharged from his teaching career. Not a single issue was mentioned in Boyle's 1998 Order. A copy of Boyle's Order is attached as Document "G" and Davis v. Walker No. 5:97-CV-350. This case issues involved the above mentioned illegal criminal trial where Complainant was forced into a court without a charge listed against him and the Complainant was denied a lawyer at his request and was imprisoned where Not a single issue appeared in Boyle's Order. Judge Boyle committed perjury according to 18 U.S. Code Sec. 1621. Another CRIMINAL ACTION: On August 21, 2019, The Complainant attempted to file his federal lawsuit against Judge Terrence W. Boyle and did so By Statement Under Penalty of Contempt. However, the Complainant's lawsuit was blocked by Judge Boyle's, assigned judge, James Dever, who also serve on the U.S. District Court for the Eastern District of North Carolina Southern Division. Therefore, Judge James Dever acted unlawful as the judge and Lawyer to hide the criminal conduct of Judge Boyle.

Therefore, Complainant Prays for the render of action, that our judicial system would have no resemblan‹ ᴗ of that of Russian as it appears in the matter of Alexei Navalny as pleasing to this Complainant; however more important than this Complainant but for the good of Our Nation.

As a final note, Complainant provided Judge Terrence W. Boyle with a letter dated July 15, 2019, advising him of a Civil complaint would be filed against him resulting from his unlawful conduct. Judge Boyle provided no opposition to a single issue established in the said letter. Complainant hereto attach a copy of the said letter is Attached as Exhibit "K".

Robert L. Davis

Robert L. Davis, Complainant

EXHIBIT "A"

COMPLAINANT'S HAND WRITTEN MOTION FOR DISTOR WITH WALKER'S ORDER OF DENIAL WRITTEN THERE UPON

FILED
93 APR 13 PM 12:50
ROBESON COUNTY, C.S.C.

"A"

In the Superior Court
92 CRS 5565

Robert L. Davis
v.
State of North Carolina

Robert L. Davis, Defendant, moves the court pursuant to criminal case file 92 CRS 5565 in preparation for trial set tomorrow at 9:30 a.m. in superior court by Jury, on & this motion further moves the court for discovery in this matter.

This the 13th Day of April 1993

Robert L. Davis
Robert L. Davis
Pro se
40 Kensington Street
Lumberton, N.C.
28358

"B"

4/14/93 MOTION IS WITHOUT MERIT. CASE NOT WITHIN ORIGINAL JURISDICTION OF SUPERIOR COURT (15A-901) THEREFORE NO RIGHT TO DISCOVERY.

RSWALKER. R
JUDGE PRESIDING

EXHIBIT "B" WALKER'S INCRIMINAING STATEMENT TO THE JURY

(Walker) App. 2

"B"

Davis voluntarily went with the officers to the police department and there from, went voluntarily to the Magistrate's office to -- to appear before the Magistrate; under those circumstances no arrest was made and no arrest warrant was required under the law of the State of North Carolina.

All right, Mr. Davis, go ahead.

MR. DAVIS: All right. Let me continue.

You also heard in testimony that Mr. Ward stated that he did, in fact, issue a -- an arrest warrant while I was at the Magistrate's office. He stated that. You heard it in the testimony.

Ladies and gentlemen, you heard also placed (sic) by the State that Jamie Floyd said -- I've been to the doctor's office; I've been sick; I've stayed out of school a whole lot.

Why didn't the State bring in evidence -- by showing a record of attendance -- a record of absentees and a record that she had been to a doctor's office?

And those days ought to parallel; shouldn't they?

But the State didn't bring any.

You heard Phillip Floyd, the father, who sit there and said he had -- that he could provide me with all the -- the bills. Do you remember hearing that?

But one thing he failed to do, he failed to say that he would provide it to the jury and to the Court. He failed to tell you that.

EXHIBIT "C" JAMIE FLOYD PERJURY ON JURY STAND

Page 1

"C"

page 4

Exhibit

Dr Parker:

Mar 31
Apr 6
29
30
May 27

5 absences for games Floyd

b. curt

Ranager

4-29-93

Total year absences attached.

Ranager

AS OF 05 JUN 92

Exhibit "C"

Page 2 — page 3

NAME	: JAIME		STUDENT NUMBER	: 3200081
SURNAME	: FLOYD		STUDENT ID	:
ADDRESS	: 32 KENSINGTON STREET		DIVISION CODE	: 10-G
	28358		GRADE CODE	: 10
			SEX CODE	: F
			ETHNIC CODE	: WHTE
RESIDES	: Mr & Mrs PHILLIP MICHAEL FLOYD		PHONE	: 919 671-0562

SCH MON	1	2	3	4	5	6	7	8	9	10	11	12	13	14	15	16	17	18	19	20	MEM	PRS	ABS
							--SCHOOL DAY--														--SUMMARY--		
1	E1																				20	20	0
2																					20	20	0
3									1	1											20	18	2
4					1	1	1	1													20	16	4
5										1	1										20	18	2
6																					20	20	0
7								1									1				20	18	2
8	1												1	1							20	17	3
9													1								20	19	1
10	XX	XX	XX	XX	XX	XX	XX	XX	XX	XX	XX	XX	XX	XX	XX	XX	XX	XX	XX	XX	0	0	0
																			TOTALS		180	166	14

FLOYD JAIME 10F
32000 HR:10-G ADVR:

2	ENG.II-H	90	1.0
2	SPANISH I	93	1.0
2	GEOMETRY	91	1.0
2	BIOLOGY-H	87	1.0
2	W. HISTORY-H	84	1.0
2	KEYBOARDING	91	1.0

ABS:14.0 TARDY:1
RANK:

	GPA	CREDITS
CURRENT	89.333	6.0
CUM	89.333	6.0

PROMOTED (CHECK ONE) : YES______ NO______ TO GRADE______

SCHOOL TRANSFERRED TO : ____________________

ADDRESS : ____________________

____

DATE RECORDS FORWARDED: ____________

TEACHER/PRINCIPAL SIGNATURE : ____________________

EXHIBIT "D" LUMBERTON POLICE OFFICE DON WARD'S PERJURY BEFORE THE COURT AND UNDER THE OATH HIS OFFICE

THE COURT: YOU MAY CROSS-EXAMINE, MR. DAVI

* * * *

CROSS-EXAMINATION BY MR. DAVIS

Q. MR. WARD, DID YOU OBTAIN A--AN--AN ARREST WARRANT THAT NIGHT?
A. YES, SIR, I DID.
Q. DID YOU ISSUE AN ARREST WARRANT?
A. WHEN I GOT TO THE MAGISTRATE'S OFFICE THAT NIGHT, THERE WAS ONE ISSUED.
Q. WHO DID YOU ISSUE AN ARREST WARRANT TO?
A. THE WARRANT WAS TAKEN OUT ON ROBERT DAVIS.
Q. WHO DID YOU ISSUE THE WARRANT TO, MR. WARD?
A. I DIDN'T ISSUE A WARRANT TO ANYBODY. THE WARRANT WAS ISSUED TO ME BY THE MAGISTRATE ON ROBERT DAVIS, AND IT WAS SERVED ON ROBERT DAVIS.
Q. WHEN DID YOU SERVE A WARRANT?
A. AFTER IT WAS OBTAINED.
Q. DO YOU HAVE A COPY OF THE WARRANT THAT WAS OBTAINED AND ISSUED?
A. NO, SIR, I DON'T.
Q. WHY DON'T YOU HAVE ONE, MR. WARD?
A. IT'S NOT STANDARD PROCEDURE FOR US TO KEEP A COPY OF TH: WARRANT.
Q. THE FACT OF IT IS YOU NEVER ISSUED A WARRANT, ISN'T THA' RIGHT?

EXHIBIT "E" JUDGE TERRENCE ACTING AS JUDGE AND LAEYER

EXHIBIT "E" Judge Terrance under perjury acted as Judge and Attorney protecting Unlawful Russell G. Walker

"B" "E"

IN THE UNITED STATES DISTRICT COURT
FOR THE EASTERN DISTRICT OF NORTH CAROLINA
SOUTHERN DIVISION

No. 7:98-CV-128-BO(1)

ROBERT L. DAVIS, Plaintiff, v. THE PUBLIC SCHOOLS OF ROBESON COUNTY, BOARD OF EDUCATION, in its official capacity; DOUGLAS Y. YONGUE, in his official and individual capacities; TOMMY D. SWETT, in his official and individual capacities; BETH WILLIAMSON, in her official and individual capacities; ABNER HARRINGTON, in his official and individual capacities; MIKE SMITH, in his official and individual capacities; PAUL BROOKS, in his official and individual capacities; ROBERT DEESE, in his official and individual capacities; and BERRY HARDING, in his official and individual capacities, Defendants.	)	<u>ORDER</u>

This matter is before the Court on a number of motions: Defendants' Motion to Dismiss, Plaintiff's motion for recusal, Plaintiff's "Motion for Judicial action on Motion to Recuse," Plaintiff's "Motion to Rescind Orders Extending Time," Defendants' motion for a protective order regarding discovery, and cross-motions for sanctions, among others. After full consideration, and for the reasons stated below, this Court will deny Plaintiff's motion for recusal, deny Plaintiff's Motion for Sanctions, grant Defendants' Motion for Sanctions in part, and grant Defendants' Motion to Dismiss. These actions will serve to moot all other pending motions in this matter.

BACKGROUND

Plaintiff Robert Lee Davis ("Davis") has filed a number of state and federal lawsuits since he was convicted of indecent exposure[1] in the Robeson County, North Carolina, General Court of Justice.[2] In his most recent litigation before this Court, Plaintiff was ordered to show cause why he should not be sanctioned pursuant to Rule 11 of the Federal Rules of Civil Procedure. While this Court declined to impose sanctions at that time, it did explicitly reserve the right to impose sanctions in the future should Plaintiff continue his pattern of harassing and vexatious lawsuits.

ANALYSIS

This Court must first consider Plaintiff's "Motion to Recuse Terrence W. Boyle District Judge." Plaintiff bases this motion on his ongoing lawsuit which names each United States District Court Judge in the Eastern District of North Carolina as a defendant.[3] Despite Plaintiff's ongoing lawsuit, he fails to put forward any tenable allegation of bias or prejudice against this Court or the undersigned Judge.[4] Plaintiff's motion seeking recusal is without merit and will be denied.

This Court now reaches Defendants' Motion to Dismiss. Defendants properly point out

---

[1] Plaintiff was convicted of indecent exposure in violation of North Carolina General Statute § 14-190.9 by a jury on April 15, 1993. This conviction led to Plaintiff's dismissal as a public school teacher.

[2] Plaintiff's litigation history was detailed in an order dismissing a prior civil rights claim. Davis v. Walker, No. 5:97-CV-350-H (E.D.N.C. June 25, 1997).

[3] Davis v. Walker, et al. (Case No. 7:98-CV-116 E.D.N.C.)

[4] Plaintiff attempts to argue that his vexatious lawsuit filed naming every Judge in the Eastern District of North Carolina as a Defendant forces all of the named Judges to be disqualified from hearing any other litigation he has filed. This argument is facially invalid. Attempting to disqualify Judges by filing lawsuits against them is an inappropriate litigation tactic, and this Court will not encourage such tactics by allowing them to succeed. The undersigned Judge is not a party to the suit at bar and has no bias or prejudice in this matter. Plaintiff's motion seeking recusal does not meet the standard set by 28 U.S.C. § 144.

for Sanctions is granted insofar as it requests such an injunction on further filings by Plaintiff. However, Defendant's Motion for Sanctions will be denied insofar as it requests payment of costs and fees.

Thus, for the reasons given above, and after full consideration, Plaintiff's motion seeking recusal of the undersigned Judge is DENIED; Defendants' Motion to Dismiss is GRANTED; Plaintiff's Motion for Sanctions is DENIED; and Defendants' Motion for Sanctions is GRANTED in part and DENIED in part. Plaintiff Robert L. Davis is hereby permanently ENJOINED from filing, commencing, or attempting to initiate any new lawsuit, action, proceeding, or matter in this Federal District Court without first obtaining leave of this Court to so proceed, as described above. The Clerk of this Court will take such actions as are necessary to implement the pre-filing injunction described above.

SO ORDERED.

This 17th day of December, 1998.

TERRENCE W. BOYLE
CHIEF UNITED STATES DISTRICT JUDGE

Deputy Clerk

Exhibit “F” POLICE OFFICER DON WARD LIED UNDER OATH

Agency Name: Lumberton Police Dept.

ORI: NC 0780100

INCIDENT/INVESTIGATION REPORT F

"DOCUMENT A"

OCA: 18-34752

Date / Time Reported: Month 09 | Day 07 | Yr. 2018 | Time 1825 Hrs. (S M T W T F S — F circled)

#	Crime / Incident(s)	Attempt / Complete	At Found	Last Known Secure
#1	Call for service	☑ Complete	Month 09, Day 07, Yr 2018, Time 1530 Hrs (F circled)	Month 09, Day 07, Yr 2018, Time 1500 Hrs. (F circled)
#2	Crime Incident	☐ Attempt ☐ Complete	Location of Incident: 410 Kensington Drive, Lumberton NC	Offense Tract: B2
#3	Crime Incident	☐ Attempt ☐ Complete	Premise Type: residence	Victim Residence Type: ☒ Single Family ☐ Multi Family

How Attacked or Committed: by threatening to arrest subject

Forcible: ☐ Yes ☒ No ☐ N/A

Weapon / Tools: mouth

# of Victims: 1

Type: ☒ Person ☐ Business ☐ Society ☐ Government ☐ Financial Institute ☐ Religious ☐ L.E. Officer Line of Duty ☐ Other/Unk

Injury: ☒ None ☐ Minor ☐ Loss of Teeth ☐ Broken Bones ☐ Severe Lacerations ☐ Internal ☐ Unconscious ☐ Other Major

Drug/Alcohol Use: ☐ Yes ☒ No ☐ Unknown ☐ N/A

	Victim/Business Name (Last, First, Middle)	Victim of Crime #	DOB / Age	Race	Sex	Relationship To Offender	Resident Status
V1	Davis, Robert	1	12/2/1942 / 75	B	M	UNK	☒ Resident ☐ Non-Resident ☐ Unknown

Home Address: 410 Kensington Street, Lumberton, NC 28358

Home Phone: 910-734-7359

Employer Name/Address:

Business Phone:

YYR	Make	Model	Style	Color	Lic/Lis	Vin

CODES: V - Victim (Denote V2, V3) O - Owner (if other than victim) R - Reporting Person (if other than victim)

Type: ☐ Person ☐ Business ☐ Society ☐ Government ☐ Financial Institute ☐ Religious ☐ L.E. Officer Line of Duty ☐ Other/Unknown

Code	Name (Last, First, Middle)	Victim of Crime #	DOB / Age	Race	Sex

Home Address:

Home Phone:

Employer Name/Address:

Business Phone:

Type: ☐ Person ☐ Business ☐ Society ☐ Government ☐ Financial Institute ☐ Religious ☐ L.E. Officer Line of Duty ☐ Other/Unknown

Code	Name (Last, First, Middle)	Victim of Crime #	DOB / Age	Race	Sex

Home Address:

Home Phone:

Employer Name/Address:

Business Phone:

L - Lost S - Stolen R - Recovered D - Damaged Z - Seized B - Burned C - Counterfeit / Forged F - Found

(Check "OJ" column if recovered for other jurisdiction)

Victim #	CC	Status	Value	OJ	QTY	Property Description	Make/Model	Serial Number

Number of Vehicles Stolen: 0

Number Vehicles Recovered: 0

Officer Name: T. Carter | ID#: 30207 | Officer Signature: T. Carter | Supervisor Signature: [signature]

Complainant Signature:

Case Status: ☐ Further Investigation ☒ Inactive ☐ Closed/Cleared ☐ Closed/Leads Exhausted

Case Disposition: ☐ Unfounded ☐ Juvenile/No Custody ☐ Extradition Declined ☐ Cleared by Arrest ☐ Refuse to Cooperate ☐ Cleared by Arrest by Another Agency ☐ Death of Offender ☐ Prosecution Declined

DCI-600A

ABOUT THE AUTHOR

The author is strictly thoughtful and direct about his Country, the United States of American. Therefore, his production of this Book is not his basic concern about himself. During his years of his youth, he set his mind to enter with the thought of taking his major in the area of history and Political Science.

Because of the author's profoundly thoughtful characteristics, he completed his undergraduate and master's degrees and pursued toward seeking his PhD. However, the Author was in close range toward reaching his goal toward his PhD with good academic standing when, unfortunately, he came in contact of injustice rained upon him by those named persons discussed in this book. Even though the Author's pursuit for his PhD was miserable, terminated by the very people who are appointed to uphold the Constitutions of our States and Nation in protecting the American People's Liberties but instead waged treasonous acts upon the Constitution of the United States, which brought more hurt on this author than that of bring his pursuit to an end regarding his PhD. Nevertheless, the author was blessed in his pursuit to acquire his educational goals to include the institutions as follows: Riverside High School, Franklin County, Louisburg, North Carolina; Shaw University, Raleigh, North Carolina. Yes, area of Study: History; graduate —Appalachian State University, Boone, North Carolina, Area of Study, Educational Leadership; Duke University, Durham, North Carolina, Area of Study, Ministerial Course of Study; and Trinity Theological Seminary, Newburgh, Indiana, Area of Study, PhD Program in Pastoral Leadership.

Further, the author as a young lad dreamed that at some point in his life he would travel to foreign countries. His dreams and wishes came to fruition: in April 1977, he was selected by the Friends of American Tours, where he traveled to the then-Soviet Union, which included a visit to Finland, and in July 1982, he was selected to participate in the Fulbright-Hays Fellowship

Program where he traveled to Pakistan for purpose to study the culture and Islamic Republic of that country. During which time he visited Istanbul, Turkey, London, and Germany.

www.ingramcontent.com/pod-product-compliance
Lightning Source LLC
LaVergne TN
LVHW011519200926
848484LV00001B/67

* 9 7 9 8 8 8 5 2 7 1 4 1 7 *